THE SILENCE OF CLOUDS

ISLA NUTBROWN

NUTBROOK BOOKS

A NUTBROOK PAPERBACK

First published in 2013 by Nutbrook Books

Copyright © 2013 Isla Nutbrown

ISBN: 978-0-9576129-0-7

For Nick

CHAPTER ONE
THE EXHIBITION

COVENT GARDEN, LONDON, ENGLAND

15 SEPTEMBER 2001

Covent Garden was vibrant as usual. Bizet's Carmen echoed round the piazza as a pretty young opera student performed her repertoire. Tourists gathered round while she busked. Others sat at tables laughing and talking enthusiastically, their ice creams melting in the mid-September sun. This was my favourite time of year in the city: the school holidays were over and the day trippers had dwindled. The busy buzz of summer had been replaced by cooler days and the golden light of autumn.

Over the past year Covent Garden had become a second home to me. Three days a week I took the tube from the forgotten wasteland of Mile End to the grandiose hub of Theatreland. In amongst the tourists and restaurants, next to the piazza, was a crumbling listed building, home to The Exhibition Market. Three days a week I worked for a friend, a lively entrepreneur, who owned a stall selling lampshades and mobiles. On each of these mornings I would clamber up a ladder, careful to avoid the missing rung, and then turn on the lamps. Once the stall was set up I'd run over to Frank's greasy café, order a coffee, chat briefly with the owner, whose charm was as legendary as the time he spent inside, run back to the stall, and wait for the bustle of the customers.

These mornings were always leisurely and most of the time was spent talking to Sal, my new, dear friend from the tea shop. Kindly and warm, dramatic and strong, Sal was a gold mine of local history – being a local herself. Market life was in her blood. Her father had owned a stall when The Exhibition had been a vegetable market and her grandfather had been a trader when the stalls had been in the piazza outside. But the most romantic of all the markets to which Covent Garden had been a home was the flower market. Sal's great-grandma, Lillian, had been a real-life Eliza Doolittle. Every day at half past five, Lilly left her house in Leather Lane, walked down the Strand past the Old Justice Courts, and arrived at the flower market. Quickly she gathered up all the flowers the traders had dropped and tied them into bundles, and then sold them on to the wealthy.

Usually I loved listening to Sal's stories and the days often flew by, but this particular day seemed like a long one. Customers had been demanding and rude and there hadn't been any respite, so after the market had closed we sought some solace in a traditional little pub with wooden beams and lovers' booths, overlooking the square where a busker was swallowing fire. The wine flowed and I sat back and pictured the piazza as it might once have looked. I saw horses pulling carriages full of finely dressed couples, clip clopping over cobbled streets; the privileged making their way to the theatre, the less so displaying their wears of roses, carnations, lilacs, and lilies. I wondered which plays they were on their way to see – a heart-stopping melodrama full of cloaks and daggers, or a wry look at life, an Oscar Wilde perhaps. Here we were in the heart of theatre land with barely a play in sight; the musicals for day trippers were now centre stage. Sal spoke, bringing me back to the here and now.

'If Philipus badgers me one more time about that bloody rent, I'll swing for him,' she complained. 'How many times do I have to tell him before he gets it into his thick head? I've paid till the end of the month?' Her accent was a strong Holborn accent, slightly different from the East End accent I heard all around me where I lived at Mile End. Philipus was the Market Manager, Greek with brown spaniel eyes, black hair, and a loud booming voice. He spent his days weaving through the stalls, collecting the rent, sorting out squabbles, and chasing the occasional thief.

'Some days I wish I could take down the lights, shut up shop, and never come back,' said Sal.

The market was still a new experience for me but Sal had been there fourteen years. The traders' faces were no longer new to her and the stories of their lives she'd heard a thousand times before. Even Marcus's tales – they kept me entertained for hours – Sal had long since tired of. Marcus was a handsome Iranian lace seller and owned the stall next to mine. We'd dance through the aisles to tinny tannoy music and top up our coffee with cheap shots of brandy. He was affectionately known as my Persian Prince. I would have happily danced off into the sunset with Marcus but Marcus was gay and no amount of lipstick or brandy could persuade him to be otherwise. So I settled for friends.

'I don't know why you don't go and find another job,' Sal said as she poured me more wine.

I couldn't care if I were rich or poor – this was the happiest I had been for years. I had struggled hard to reach this state of mind, but Sal didn't know how I'd felt before or about my past. She knew I'd been an actress, but that was really all she knew, and for now that was all I wanted to tell her. Sal often advised me to find another job, but despite her complaining about The Exhibition, she secretly loved the everyday dramas that market life brought and always had her ears to the ground for who had said what to whom. The humid heat caused tempers to snap and there was seldom any breeze beneath the roof to cool the rising tensions, but as well as traders arguing, there were also traders falling in love and that's what I loved about the market. People were open with their emotions. Years spent communicating, haggling, and being on show left the traders unafraid to express themselves and how they felt and what they thought was never suppressed. Reserved they certainly weren't. They reminded me of actors in many ways, and that's why I felt so at home amongst them. Philipus, with his huge booming voice and forlorn brown eyes could have stepped straight off the stage of the Pantheon and into the aisles of this market.

As Sal refilled our glasses with cold white wine she looked at me thoughtfully. 'Why don't you go back into acting?' It was as though she'd been reading my mind. The fact was, I was still in the process of rebuilding my life and the person who had once strode onto a stage or tried to bring a character to life on screen didn't feel like me anymore. Acting required immense confidence and I was still struggling to find that, but the market was helping me. Dealing with customers, working with spirited people, and feeling the community of market life gave me the elements I needed to learn to trust life again. The explanation for why my confidence was so severely shattered was too long and much too difficult to discuss over a glass of wine. I gave Sal a standard vague reply.

'You know how it is. Acting's an up-and-down profession.'

'Well if I were you, I'd get back on the up side. Sharpish! You don't want to be stuck down here all your life!'

But in my mind I wasn't stuck. In fact I felt the opposite. My time at the market, with its colourful people and their interwoven lives, had given me a new lease of life and for the first time in a long while I not only felt content, I felt like I belonged again. Sal didn't know the sanctuary that they, the traders, had given me because Sal was unaware of the isolation I'd felt over the past three years.

I looked out past the square, over the early evening revellers, beyond the wrought iron roof of The Exhibition and out into the sky. The air had the scent and feel of autumn. I pulled my coat tighter around me, lost in my world as my thoughts reverted back to three years before, back to South America. Yet as quickly as those memories came to mind, I forced them away again, lit a cigarette, and changed the subject, moving the conversation on to one of Sal's favourite topics – the state of middle-aged men's hair. To this day, I have no idea why Sal was obsessed with this particular aspect of men's grooming, but she was and still is, and men's hair, or often the lack of it, could keep her amused and talking for hours.

'I see Davey's gone a few shades darker,' I offered.

Sal laughed. 'Bless him! He was silver last week – now look at him. He's browner than a chestnut. Does he think no one will notice?' Davey, a trader in the daytime and a taxi-driver by night, was a statuesque, handsome man with a soft London accent and eyes that smiled through even the coldest days. 'Have you ever met his brother?' I hadn't. 'Well, he's as charming as Davey but ten years younger. Married a barrister. Still got his own coloured hair, mind you.'

For the next half hour Sal told me the ins and outs of the two brothers' lives as the sky turned from dark blue to starlit. The wine bottle was empty.

'Early start again tomorrow. Shall we call it a night?' Sal asked.

The wine had worked its magic; our moods were quietly elated. Both of us decided to head back to our beds, but once I was alone walking down the Strand, past weary tourists and night-time thrill-seekers, my heart felt heavy, weighed down with the memories of three years ago. The underground was hot, the tube doors opened, and I sat with my own thoughts as we passed beneath St Paul's station, Bank, and Liverpool Street. The journey stopped at Mile End but my thoughts continued. I passed the kebab shops, bus stops, and worn-out terraced houses. The thoughts were still with me as I entered my front door. Suli, my grey tabby cat, appeared to be as hungry as I was. Together we ate and we watched TV. I went to bed but couldn't sleep. I got up, poured a glass of wine, smoked some cigarettes, and thought about my time in South America and the effect it had had on my life. Suli drifted off to sleep beside me, but I stayed awake until morning.

CHAPTER TWO
THE THIRD MAN

OTOVALO, ECUADOR, SOUTH AMERICA

13 DECEMBER 1998

The policeman hit the keys of the typewriter as the fan turned in its rhythm, in the corner of the room. It occasionally jarred as the fan blade caught. Outside the sun was shining. It was morning and the heat was comfortable and fresh. Inside the interview room it was dark and dank. The whitewashed police station stood one storey high and was manned by two policemen. The older sat in front of me behind a peeling Formica desk.

His brown eyes boasted dark circles and beneath his armpits his shirt showed heavy sweat stains. Sara, my friend, was in the room next door, recounting her version of the events. Andréa, in her mid-thirties, energetic, and the owner of the hostel where we were staying, had come along with me to translate. We'd known her only three days, the same amount of time we'd been in Otovalo. Currently she was pacing the room.

'Name: Isla Nutbrown. Age: 27. Occupation: Actress ...'

The policeman repeated 'Actress?' with obvious interest. He asked Andréa some other questions. It was the first time I'd seen the man animated. Up until now, he'd shown no interest in the events that had happened the day before.

'Are you in films?' Andréa asked me. 'They want to know if they can see you on the television.'

'Is this at all relevant?' I asked. She told the policeman to carry on with the statement.

'At what time did you leave the hotel?'

'11.15 a.m.'

'And at what time did you arrive at the top of the mountain?'

'11.45 a.m. We took a taxi up there.'

The taxi had been light blue, the same colour as the nearing midday sky. As we drove further and higher up the mountain, the views expanded all around us – spring green countryside, ploughed brown fields, and small mountain villages. We paid the taxi driver and got out of the car. The silence settled upon us.

'Was there anyone else up on the mountain when you got there?'

'Yes. As the taxi was dropping us off, three or four walkers were heading back down the road we'd just driven up.'

The policemen pressed down the keys laboriously, typing in

the information.

'Apart from the people you saw, were you alone up there?'

'Obviously not,' I replied. His indifference was beginning to irritate me.

'So what happened next? After you were dropped off by this taxi driver?'

'He drove away and we began to hike around the lakes. After about half an hour we stopped and sat down by the water. I think we ate something and drank some juice that we had in our bags.'

I remember Sara and I sat looking out across the hills, gazing in silence, as we absorbed our surroundings. This was our tenth day in Ecuador and our third day in the Andes. Up until now we'd spent our time in Quito, the capital, acclimatising to the altitude and adapting to our new culture. But it was here, amongst the farmers, and mountain towns and villages, it felt as though we'd finally arrived in South America.

'We stopped for half an hour and then carried on exploring. A blue pick-up truck passed us and pulled up a few yards in front. Two men sat in the back, in the open rear, and one man was in the driver's seat. One of the men in the back asked us if we wanted a lift up the steep part of the road that ran to the peak of the mountain. I didn't like him. He had an arrogant air about him.'

'Describe him to me,' the policeman said. 'His hair, his eyes?'

'He was probably five feet eight. Medium build. Mid-brown coloured hair, dark brown Mediterranean skin – weathered. Most likely in his early thirties. His left front tooth was gold.'

'He must be wealthy,' Andréa observed.

The policeman shrugged and then mustered up enough energy to nod his head.

'What was he wearing?'

'A shirt. A dark green shirt and blue denim tight-legged jeans. He was casual – smart almost and stank of aftershave.'

'You said there was another man. Describe him.'

'Small and stocky. He didn't look Spanish – not like the other one. He looked Eastern, maybe Mongolian. He had a wide, large jaw and jet black eyes. Ugly. That's what I remember. He was very ugly. His clothes were the same. Casual light blue denim jeans, a white t-shirt – very tight. He was trying to show off his muscles.'

'And the driver?'

'I didn't see the driver.'

'So, what happened next?'

'We told them we didn't want a lift and they drove off.' Suddenly I had felt kind of disconcerted; concerned we might be alone on the mountain with these three men. I asked Sara her thoughts, and she told me we'd be fine. There were probably other people up here, she said. The lakes are one of the area's most popular spots. That was that. I didn't think about the blue truck again.

'We walked higher up the mountain, and the road curved around the second lake and got noticeably steeper. It was mid-afternoon by now and the sun was at its hottest. The clouds were now way beneath us, grey and white, stretching out like a threatening sea. We stopped again for water and took off our jackets, tying them round our waists.'

Sara taught me a psychological game, involving a long, imaginary rope tied around the rocky peak, to help us climb the steepest part of the mountain. Together we picked up the 'rope' and pulled it through our hands, heaving our way up the road. Magically it helped.

'What if we try flying?' I suggested. Flapping our arms like wings, we made our way further up the road, laughing as our feet kicked up stones and dust that whirled like miniature sandstorms as we ran. I had a sudden rush of euphoria – we were exuding happiness from deep down in our bellies, happy to be free from everyone and everything. I refused to tell the policeman any of this, not only because it wasn't relevant to our statement, but because I didn't want to reveal to him how childlike we could be. I didn't want him to think we were naive little girls. We weren't. I knew instinctively how difficult it was going to be to have this case taken seriously by the police. I had to show him strength. Ecuador is a patriarchal country with a macho climate. We were well and truly in a man's world. Anything that weakened our statement I had to omit.

'The road evened out again and we carried on walking – we'd nearly reached the peak of the mountain. Suddenly a man's voice cried out like a war cry. Before we had time to think, he'd jumped down in front of us from the rocks above. He was holding a gun – it was pointing right at us.'

I lost all ability to comprehend the space around me. It was as though I was watching a film in slow motion. I could see what was unfolding before my eyes but I couldn't make sense of it. It was too disturbing to enter my psyche. For a split second I was in denial, or deep shock, but as adrenalin began to pump around my body it alerted me to the reality of the situation and every thought came crashing in at once.

There's a man in front of me. He's holding a gun. It's pointing right at us. This is an ambush. We're being attacked. This isn't happening. This can't be real. Please God, tell me this isn't happening. This only happens in films. This doesn't happen in real life, this doesn't happen to me.

Before I could think of any way out, hands grabbed hold of me. Two other men had leaped out from the long grass. One dragged me away from the road while the other held a gun against my neck. I could feel its cold barrel break my skin. They pulled us further and further into the grass. One other thought streamed through my consciousness: I'm going to die.

'And these were the same three men who were in the truck?' the policeman asked.

'Yes. I recognised them instantly. Their blue pick-up truck was parked off the road in the grass. They'd been waiting for us.'

'Did you fight them?'

I found this question insulting and accusatory. Perhaps he was asking out of morbid curiosity. He was no longer indifferent to my situation; his interest had been ignited by the drama I was relating to him, or perhaps I was being defensive because the question made me feel uncomfortable. I hadn't fought them and this haunted me. Was I weak for not kicking and screaming? Would the outcome have been different if I had? But there was only one thought that had been going through my head and that was that I had to survive. I couldn't die now. One false move on my part and they might retaliate by pulling the trigger of the gun that was still pressed firmly against my neck. I was a split second away from death.

'Would you fight with a gun pointing against your head?' I asked.

'Are you okay?' Andréa asked. 'Do you want to carry on? We can go and get a coffee in the town – come back in half an hour or so?'

'No, let's carry on.'

I wanted to relay the statement as quickly as possible, getting it over and done with. The policeman lit another cigarette.

'Sara was being dragged away from me. I called out her name but they stopped me from shouting by gagging my mouth with tape.'

'They tied tape around your mouth?'

'Yes. Thick blue gaffer tape – and then they taped it round my eyes.'

The bounding of my eyes and mouth signified the beginning of the nightmare, not the end. I realised they were not here just to steal my possessions; they were going to abuse me and psychologically torment me.

'Next they tied my wrists together, in front of me, with some kind of electrical wire.'

I stopped for a glass of water. The policeman put out his cigarette. I took a deep breath and spoke quickly and precisely, trying to talk over the emotions I was feeling. The man sat in front of me had no understanding or compassion for my situation. I refused to show him my vulnerability. In this dark, dank room I wasn't going to cry.

'One of them knocked me to the ground and onto my back while another one held me down.'

The man who'd pushed me began to pull at the buttons of my jeans, dragging them down to my ankles. Next he yanked down my pants. I was naked from the waist down. I managed to lift my head off the ground and partially I could see over the blindfold. I watched him undo his belt and the zip on his trousers. I had to see him – I needed to know where the gun was. I wanted to see which one was holding my life between his fingers. He had no gun. Instead his hands were free to make himself hard. I lay still and prayed.

If there is a God, intervene, save me.

He lay on top of me and rammed his penis inside me. I wasn't wet and it hurt, but the pain of his entering was quickly replaced by nauseating fear. The man who'd pinned down my shoulders had pushed the cold barrel of the gun into my neck again. Between them they had complete control of me – I couldn't move and I couldn't fight – the ultimate turn-on for a psychotic. The man on top of me laughed as he raped, revealing a row of yellow, stained teeth and one which was gold. He came quickly inside me and stood up next to me, buttoning his trousers and fastening his belt with a slow, deliberate swagger. A job well done. The man with the revolver got on top of me, like a fairground ride, and forced his way into me, passing the gun to the other rapist who pointed it at me as his friend rammed his penis in and out. The stench of aftershave and sweat made me sick and his ugly, leering face swirled through my stomach, causing me to retch into the gaffer tape gag. Would they shoot me once he came, or did the other man want to jump on as well?

'What about the third man? What was he doing?' asked the policeman.

'He was standing nearby.'

What I didn't tell the policeman was how I'd put my hands together in a prayer's position, fingers pointing to the sky and begging him with my actions, unable to speak.

Please don't. Don't. Please don't rape me. I can't go through it again ... please.

I repeated the words over and over in my mind and lowered my head towards my chest so I could see him over the top of the blindfold. He was staring straight ahead, not at me. Even though I couldn't see his face or read his emotions, I could sense he no longer wanted to be part of this. He was turning his back on the crime, standing away from the violation. I could feel his guilt and I clung onto it, his shame giving me hope. I was desperately praying that his conscience would burn a hole into his mind, ordering him to leave me alone, telling him to leave me alive. This man could save my life. As a girl I'd once read a book about nomads and gypsies and their powers of telepathy over hundreds of miles. I'd liked the idea – it was magical. I'd always thought it could work. I hoped right now that it would. I willed my thoughts to the third man.

Don't rape me. Don't do it. Walk away and rise above it. They want you to rape me, don't you see? It will make them feel less guilty. It will take away their shame. All the boys were in it together – it was all a bit of a laugh. But you know differently – if you rape me again and kill me, the act will never leave you. It will haunt you every day and breathe inside you for the rest of your life. Walk away and they will follow. They are weak; they have no minds of their own. Speak from your heart. Talk to them. Tell them to leave me alive.

I looked at him over the blindfold, and he was smoking a cigarette. The smoke drifted towards me, carried by the wind.

Don't rape me. Don't do it. Walk away and rise above it.

He turned around, looked straight at me with his dark brown eyes, and began to walk towards me. I'd been wrong. He had no conscience. I was going to die. This time, defeated, I closed my eyes and waited for the ordeal to be over. Lying in the grass, I imagined a white tunnel, long and luminous, with my grandparents at the end of it calling to me. I would float into the tunnel after the trigger was pulled and once again I'd be safe. The image comforted me as I waited to die. I heard his footsteps coming towards me, cutting through the long grass, and felt something on my legs. But it wasn't skin – it wasn't him. It was a soft, heavy material: my fleece. He'd covered my naked body with the fleece lying next to me.

'Vamos,' he said. (Let's go.)

The two rapists were standing a few yards behind me. I could hear them talking together in deep, jarring voices. They came over to where I was lying and pulled a silver necklace from my neck and forced the trainers off my feet. Finally they snatched back the fleece, leaving me bare again. I could hear the wind wailing as their footsteps moved through the grass, getting further and further away. A car door banged, an engine droned, and the sound of tyres crunching on gravel echoed through the air. I managed to pull down the blindfold in time to see the sky-blue pick-up truck blaze around a bend higher up the mountain. They'd finally gone. Had the third man saved my life?

'They drove away eventually,' I informed the policeman, 'after they'd robbed us.'

Andréa began to pace the room again.

'What did they take?' the policeman asked. He sounded as though I'd just told him someone had broken into my car and taken the radio or a duffle bag.

'They took my fucking dignity – you stupid fucking prick.'

His indifferent attitude finally made me crack, but he didn't react. He just stared at me and asked another question.

'He wants to know how you got down the mountain,' Andréa translated softly.

'How the fuck does he think we got back? We walked fifteen miles through the night, in the dark.'

'That's all,' he said. 'I don't need anything else.'

The statement was over. I walked out into the day, blinking through the sunlight, leaving only my words in the dark, dank room. My disillusionment and anger came along with me.

CHAPTER THREE
LOST

MOUNT MOJANDA, ECUADOR, SOUTH AMERICA
12 DECEMBER 1998

When I was a small girl I was given a present, a first edition of
The Lion the Witch and the Wardrobe. The book was worn and
its pages were tanned, but like an old hidden scroll, its weathered
look added more mystery. The gift became a portal to a private
magical kingdom. Every day, as I turned over its dusty pages, I
stepped into woods engulfed by snow and spoke to fauns and wise
old lions. The real world quickly disappeared, and while the pages
were still warm from my fingers the magic was all mine. It was
cosy in my bedroom where I read, and during the night the hands
on my bedside clock lit up in the dark and a wooden mouse in
the centre would rock in time with the beat of the tick and the

tock. Sometimes I thought it was a magical mouse on the cusp of a wave, other times a sprightly small dormouse jumping over furrows in a field.

Occasionally I'd have nightmares in my room. My worst nightmare was set in a field. A soily field with sharp pieces of corn springing up like blades, and the blades went on as far as the eye could see, divided by brown leafless hedges and wooden bare fences. Here, in this field, I was being held down by a huge man who force-fed me worms over and over again. His hair was matted and he had soup on his chin, which dripped down onto his thick, khaki green anorak where the lining was ripped and the pockets were torn. He opened my mouth and fed me worm after worm. I couldn't run or hide. I didn't know why he was doing this. I wanted him to stop and I cried and cried, but gradually I realised I could do something. I could open my eyes. I could open them up and the whole thing would stop. I opened them. Eyes open wide. I was back in my bedroom, hushed by moonlight and the mouse which was still gently swinging with every tick-tock. I ran into my parent's room and crawled into their bed and my mum would sing me a lullaby. Soon I was asleep again. In my mind, nightmares were the colour of khaki.

One bright December day, the Andes, steeped in magic and folklore, turned from daylight into a nightmare. But in actual fact, it wasn't a nightmare. On this particular day, as the sun dazzled the sky, there wasn't a nightmare at all. The day was as real as the earth where I sat on my knees with my jeans around my ankles and my hands held tightly together in a prayer position. And the reality was, I couldn't open my eyes and make it stop because a blindfold was pressing them shut, and all I could hear was the wind rushing across the peak. And then there was silence. The deep staccato voices had stopped.

The wind rushes again, an engine revs, and tyres crunch on a gravel road. I pull down the blindfold, just in time to see a sky-blue truck disappear around a bend, higher up the mountain. I blink my eyes, trying to dislodge a residue of glue from my eyelashes. I open them up as wide as I can, but there isn't a mouse tick-tocking by my bed or a room to run to for a lullaby.

I pull up my trousers and pants; there isn't any time to think. I have to find my friend.

'Sara, Sara ... where are you?' I shout. There hasn't been a gun shot. She must be alive. 'Sara, Sara ... where the fuck are you?'

'I'm here, I'm here.' A small voice cuts through the wind. Sara is thirty metres away, crawling slowly towards me on her knees. Her hands are bound in front of her. She is barely visible, engulfed by the long khaki grass. I stand up and jump through the blades, over clumps of soil.

'Are you okay ... you're okay?' I ask as I run towards her.

'Yes, I'm alright,' she says. 'Let me undo you.'

Sara unties the wire which is binding my wrists together. Her fingers fumble. I do the same for her and throw the wire to the ground where it coils in the grass like a poisonous snake. If this day were in a film, now would be the scene where Sara and I grab hold of each other and sob in each other's arms, but in actual fact I don't feel anything. Like a bare tree in winter, all life has been stripped from me. My bones are with me but the rest of me has left.

'Did they rape you?' I ask her.

'No. Did they rape you?'

'Yes.' There is silence ... 'Sara, I don't know what to do,' I say.

'I do. We need to find our stuff.'

Sara moves around me like water as she searches for her belongings that have been thrown from her bag. The only thing she finds is a small address book, shiny and silver, with a rainbow on the front.

'Let's find your stuff. It'll be around here somewhere.' Sara has always been a practical person, but her lucid rationality now seems incongruous. We're on the peak of a mountain and her friend has been raped. She begins to look through the grass, squashing it down with her small, shoeless feet. 'Is this your bag? Here, look! I've got your bag.'

Sara holds up a small blue knapsack – empty and lifeless. She is now a few yards away from me and the wind has slipped in between.

'Don't go so far away,' I shout, and run over to where she is standing by a patch of flattened grass. It's where the rapes took place. At her feet are two cigarette stubs and an empty water bottle. 'This is where they raped me.'

'They even drank our water, the bastards,' Sara said.

I can't understand why she is ignoring the gang rape, yet seems so angry about our water bottle. Maybe stealing our water is the final straw for Sara. A tremendous insult, spitting in the face of injury.

'I don't know what to do?' I plead.

'I know exactly what to do. We have to get back to the hostel. It's getting dark. We better go.'

She's trying to stay in control, I think. That's what she's doing. She's not ignoring gang rape; she's merely trying to maintain some control like a school teacher or a mother with a child. She's being rational and knows that someone has to be the leader.

'How are we going to get there?' I ask.

'We're going to walk down the road.'

'I can't get back on the road. What if they come back? They'll see us straight away.'

'They won't come back,' Sara says.

Panic stabs at my stomach like a pneumatic drill, making me feel sick. 'Sara, they know we're up here alone. They can track us down like fucking rabbits. They'll hunt us down with torchlights and headlights. In the morning we'll be two bodies found in the bushes, covered in blood.'

All I want to do is curl up into a ball, like a child, and make everything disappear.

'We have to move,' Sara demands. 'We have to keep our circulation going. If we don't, we'll freeze to death. We have to move right now.'

If I close my eyes it will all go away. Someone will find us in the morning and then everything will be fine. 'I'd rather freeze and die than be raped again,' I say. If we lie down and huddle up we could keep warm and it will all be alright.

'Isla, we have to start moving.'

Maybe we'll fall asleep if we cuddle up together. 'I can't go through it again. I can't go back on the road.' I am adamant. I don't understand Sara's motivation. I can't see how she can contemplate setting one foot on the road. Is she mad?

'It'll get below freezing tonight. We have to start moving.'

No, she isn't mad. She's maintaining control in a bizarre and frightening situation. The strict but fair mother, and I am the child who has to learn to trust again.

'Okay, let's move,' I say, 'but can we go down the side of the mountain instead of the road? We can climb over its rock face.'

'Okay, we can try.' Sara speaks the words softly; the mother has compromised.

We cross over the road to the other side of the mountain which leads to Otovalo and begin our descent through the grass. The further down the mountain we climb, the longer it grows. Like wading out into the sea, soon it is up to our waists. Bracken and ferns close in around us and boughs of wood sprout from the ground. We keep losing our footing, but cover much ground, and the grass feels spongy beneath our shoeless feet.

'Sara, I have to stop for a while,' I say. 'There's something I've got to do.'

I sit down on a low, gnarly branch that sprouts from a half bush, half tree. The wind blows into my face as I take off my jeans and pull off my pants, wet from the two men's semen. I throw them as far away from me as I possibly can and pull up my trousers. We carry on down the mountain, faltering through the grass. Sara doesn't speak and neither do I. The bushes are unkind with their thorns and the terrain has become harsher.

We carry on climbing over the rock, but the rock is neither smooth nor fair and soon we come to an overhang, and the only way down is to jump. We stand on the hard grey ledge and stare at the plateau below.

'It's too far,' Sara says and she walks away from the edge without any hesitation.

'But there's grass and bushes below. They might catch our fall.'

'And they might not and we could break our backs.'

'Let's do it,' I say. 'Let's try.'

I have an overwhelming urge to jump off the edge, like gamblers stacking all that they own on red. There is nothing left to lose. Spin the wheel. Take the leap. It is rash and brave, desperate and sad. I can feel the urge to jump rise inside me.

'Let's go,' Sara says, and she pulls me away.

I have no choice but to turn around and begin the descent down to the road. We scramble in silence over the khaki grass and gauze and green bushes, occasionally slipping on mounds of hidden soil. When we finally reach the road the sky has turned black, but the lights of Otovalo glitter in the distance like beacons of hope, gold and amber, and warm. I can reach those lights, I think to myself, and I will. I can and I will and it won't be long before I'm sitting in the safety of the hotel bar. The image of a cool glass in one hand and a cigarette in the other anchor my thoughts to ordinariness.

I step out onto the road and begin the fifteen-mile walk home. Back to the lights. Lights that shine on travellers as they meet and drink and dance. Suddenly the will to get home feels as strong and as bright as the stars above. Their light glistens on the road and I can see for a few feet ahead, but the undergrowth beside me falls into darkness and anything or anyone could be hiding there, yet I try my hardest not to think about the dark and instead I look down at my feet and think only about them. Like a Zen Buddhist meditating, I concentrate on my footsteps. One foot in front of the other, over and over again. This is the action that will take me home.

I begin to lose myself in my mantra and the vastness of the mountains and when I do the fear softens and calmness seeps into my soul. But the peace seems short-lived, and when an animal cries out, disturbed from its sleep, it sends terror right through me like an electric shock, inducing panic that freezes me dead in my tracks. And the Andes are no longer my friends, but are hostile and dangerous, impervious to man.

'Sara, I'm frightened. I can't do this anymore. I can't move. I just can't do it.' I stop in my tracks on the road.

'You've done well so far,' she encourages me. 'We must have been walking for hours.'

'I want to stop. Please can we stop?'

'Let's try some small steps and see where they lead.'

'Okay,' I say, 'but please can I take hold of your hand.'

She holds my hand and coaxes me along the path, and if this were a dream, we would say to each other, 'There's no place like home' and together we'd click our heels and I'd wake up in my small childhood bed. But in reality, fear shivers through my mind, and the stones on the road cut through our socks, yet the lights of the town twinkle like Oz. Hostels and safety and beer.

I picture the bar again: homely and wooden with bright woven rugs on the wall. But then, in my mind, I see a seedier tavern where the rapists are drinking, downing shots of tequila, grabbing their glasses with hands full of sin.

'What if they start telling everyone they raped me?' I ask Sara, alarmed. 'People will know we're up here alone. Other men will drive up and rape us?'

'They won't talk,' Sara says, trying to reassure me. 'They'd be incriminating themselves.'

'Beer loosens tongues.'

'Please try not to think about it,' she says.

'Sara, I can't move.'

'You can.'

'I can't.'

'Shall I tell you a story? Something to concentrate on?' she suggests.

'Yes, tell me the story about Egypt and the beach. Remember

the beach? You went there with your friends?'

'Do you mean the cove where everyone had to leave a present?'

'Yes, that's the one.' And I began to walk.

'What do you want to know?' Sara asks, as playfully as she can.

'Tell me anything, anything at all. Who did you go with, which friends? Was the sea warm? Were there fish in it? What colour were they? Was the sand white or golden? Tell me anything, anything at all,' I spit out the words frantically.

'We all travelled together. Daphne and Natalie and me. Do you remember Natalie? She was the pretty one who surfed and ran off with an Australian sheep farmer.'

Sara holds my hand again and the moon comes out briefly from behind the cloud and the dense undergrowth shines like dew at first light.

She had first told me about the cove one night in late August, sitting in a field in the Vale of the Yorkshire Dales. The day had been warm and bright, but during the evening autumn had crept in through the late summer sky, cooling the air. There had been eight of us all together, sitting around a camp fire telling our stories as we watched the flames' shape shift, telling their own.

Sara continues, '… and the place was known as the Cove of Good Will. One day we went deep, down into the sea to look at the sharks in a rattling old cage …'

A car accelerates in the distance, and the sound of its engine ricochets around the mountains. A sick feeling hits the pit of my stomach and I begin to gasp for breath.

'Sara, they're coming back. Who else is it going to be this time? I knew they'd come back ... I told you they would.'

I throw myself off the road and into bushes, crawling through the undergrowth over anything in my way, trying to find a place to hide, somewhere where the branches might conceal the whole of me. Sara dives in after me and we hold onto each other. My heart thumps against my chest as the engine sound grows nearer and nearer.

'Their headlights will search us out,' I whisper. 'Lie flat.'

We throw ourselves on our stomachs and the twigs crack beneath us, disturbing a creature that leaps through the bushes, and our hearts nearly explode. We are sitting in silence, holding our breaths.

'Listen,' Sara whispers. 'The engine's getting quieter. It's going away. Whoever it is, they're moving away.' She's right. The sound of the car is fading and the mountains are restored to silence.

'Who do you think it was?' I demand.

'I don't know.'

'Do you think it was them?'

'No,' Sara assures me. 'It was probably some kids driving around.'

'Are you sure?' I ask.

'Yes. Whoever it was, they've gone. We're okay now.'

Sara crawls out of her hiding place, branches snap and crunch as she moves her knees over the ground, but I stay where I am.

Sara tries to coax me to move from the undergrowth. 'We must be over half way there now,' she says. 'There'll only be a few miles left. It'll be okay. I'll hold your hand.'

I crawl through the bushes and stand upon the stony road, but the sound of the engine has affected my brain; it's been scrambled by too much adrenaline. I can't make sense of anything at all. 'Sara, where are the lights? The lights in the town ... they've gone? There aren't any. Tell me where they are. They can't just disappear,' I demand.

'They're still here, but right now they're on the other side of the mountain,' she gently explains.

'I don't understand? How can a town move? A town doesn't fucking move.' I stand in the middle of the road waving my arms around, pointing at the sky, and stabbing into the darkness. 'Where are the lights? Where the fuck have they gone?'

Sara is patient and remains incredibly lucid but she seems so fragile against the backdrop of the vast rugged mountains. Formidable in their silence. 'We've been walking around the side of the mountain,' Sara explains, 'spiralling around it like a helter skelter. Sometimes we face the town and sometimes we don't. Soon we'll walk around a bend and Otovalo will be right in front of us again. The lights will come back, I promise.'

'Okay,' I say.

I don't really understand where the lights have gone, but Sara seems to know where they are, so I let her lead me onwards and hold onto her small hand and ask her to tell me a story to distract my thoughts.

'Shall I tell you a funny story?' she asks.

'Okay.'

'It's something about Ryan that you don't know.'

Ryan is Sara's ex-boyfriend.

'Really?' I'm intrigued.

'I once went to a wedding with him,' Sara says conspiratorially, 'and he drank so much alcohol that he started insulting everyone and began to bark like a dog.' I start to laugh. 'And he became such an embarrassment that my Uncle Van had to put him to bed.'

'Wow, he's a dark horse!' I am amazed. Ryan is the epitome of politeness.

And suddenly, for a moment, we are two friends on holiday sauntering back to our hotel.

'I knew Ryan and me wouldn't be together forever,' Sara says. 'I think me and Ali are far better suited – don't you?'

'I think so,' I agree. 'He's a bit more of a free spirit ... more spontaneous.'

'I just wish I could get him to commit a bit more.'

And Sara begins to expand on her favourite topic of conversation: Ali, her relationship and children, and life becomes what it was twelve hours ago. Silence ensues, as natural as the quiet of the night, and time ceases to have any meaning. It doesn't go by quickly or slowly; it just simply passes. Like those who sleep and dream, another reality has taken over. People in their houses live by the clock; here on the mountain the wind rattles the leaves when it pleases and the moon follows the sun.

Eventually we reach the lakes, the Lakes Mojanda. Three large pools expand before us, gleaming silver, catching stars. Eight hours earlier, when the sun had been shining and the sky was pure blue, this was the place where we'd stopped to rest. Dragonflies hovering, dancing like quavers on bars of music, while birds had skimmed over the water, diving for fish and pure joy. Tomorrow there'd be other travellers watching these birds on the sandy banks, and they would never know that we'd stood here during the cold dark night by the water's shore, teetering on the edge of sanity. I walk to the banks of one of the lakes to see if I can drink from it, but the silver pools are lined with moss and the water is green like the branches of the trees which enclose us.

'Look at our feet!' Sara exclaims.

Finally we can see ourselves for the very first time as the lakes reflect the moonlight. Our feet have doubled in size and blood has seeped through the soles of our socks.

'We'll have to walk on the verge,' Sara says. Next to the road, on the edge of the mountain, is a narrow grassy verge; spongy, soft, and green.

'But what if we slip and fall down the mountain?' I ask.

But Sara is already walking on the precipice, and so far her instincts have been right. I abandon the road and follow behind her like a dutiful mountain goat.

'Not long now,' Sara shouts back to me. 'The lakes are only six or seven miles from home.'

The lakes are vast and we follow them for a long time, and if this were still a film, now would be the point where I'd stop and gaze across the water and break down in tears and the lakes would be a metaphor for the pools of sorrow I carried within me. Or maybe I'd slip into the water and cleanse myself, washing away the rapists' aftershave that had seeped into my clothes, restoring my innocence. But in real life I am emotionless and the wind is the only thing I can feel as it blows across the mountain, through our hair and eyelashes towards the town below.

'Sara. Look! Do you think that's the square where all the cafes and bars are?' There's a small cluster of lights beneath us, and the town is getting nearer.

'I think so. We might only be a couple of hours away; maybe less.' And beyond the lights of the town, other lights are shining, scattered over fields; farmhouses and barn lights, places that hadn't been visible while we were standing on the peak. Now they are clear. Safety is within reach. If the rapists want to find us, time is running out.

Are they asleep by now, I wonder, or slumped in the corner of a bar? Perhaps they are ramming cocaine up their noses, getting high, riling themselves up before their return.

'Sara, will you tell me another story?' I need to think about something else.

'Of course, but we're okay now. Even our feet will be fine. Ghandi walked all across India in his bare feet, and he was fine and so shall we be.'

But my feet aren't my main concern. 'Sara, if we do get back I don't think I'll be the same again. Ever ...' But there is silence. Either Sara hasn't heard me or this time she can't find the words to reassure me.

And gradually the ground we walk upon becomes less steep and the road is now leading us to flatter plains, arable land and farms where people live and work. Soon there might be signs of life, the shadowy shapes of animals, outlines of wool and flesh. No longer will we be surrounded by grey lumps of rock that change into crouching men at the blink of an eye. And as the road flattens, it widens and becomes more like an ordinary road leading to a town, a road that will end up at a crossroads and traffic lights, a prelude to civilization.

And for the first time since leaving the peak I think I might actually soon be safe and I think Sara does too. Her voice has become looser and higher, like a bird freed from its cage, and a dog barks in the distance as though it has heard her song. Another one answers it, louder and deeper, and then a third one joins in to the chorus. Soon all three of them have emerged through the darkness. They step into our vision and sneer beneath the light of the stars. Like Helios' dogs, they growl and snarl and bark, guarding the pathway out of hell.

The largest dog, brown and muscular, displays its dominance and stands in front of the other two on its claw-like paws with its head held high. It growls and slavers, saliva dripping from its mouth with excitement as it bears its teeth. If it were a man it would be arrogant enough to have a golden tooth. Behind it is a smaller dog jumping from side to side like a boxer, anticipating its opponent's first move, while the third dog hangs further back still, its eyes watching the performance being played out in front of it, waiting for its cue to join in and attack. Its coat is black and hot breath curls through its nose and mouth like cigarette smoke. They are the guard dogs from our hostel that are chained up during the day and let loose through the night. The boxer jumps from foot to foot awaiting our next move, but we don't move a muscle, and stay as still as the fields around us.

'We can't go past them. They'll attack us straight away,' I whisper.

But Sara can smell the log fire burning in the small wooden bar and feels its flames flickering against her skin, and nothing will deter her now. But for me this chapter is over. I've walked down the mountain and can no longer walk any further. I am totally and utterly spent. The end of the night is simple: by the side of the road is a ditch, deeper than it is wide. Here in this ditch, hidden from cars, I will spend the rest of the night and wait until the dogs are back on their chains. And then I will walk back to my bed.

'They're dogs, not men,' Sara says. 'They can't pull triggers.'

I turn my back on the ditch. 'Whatever we do, we mustn't look into their eyes,' I whisper. 'They'll see it as a sign of attack.'

'Okay,' she says, 'after three?'

I nod.

'One, two, three … run!'

We run as fast as we can over stones and lumps with the wind behind us. And in the film we would have barged right through the dogs and run until we could barely breathe and the animals would be chasing us all the way, but we would be victorious and soon arrive back at the hostel, exhausted but safe. And together we would sit around the fire with woollen rugs covering our shoulders, a beer in one hand and a cigarette in the other. But in real life the dogs are too strong; their powerful paws knock us sideways and I can feel their saliva drip onto my hands. We crawl into the ditch and watch the stars fade as the sun gradually creeps back into the sky. We rub each other's hands to keep warm and flap our arms and sing songs to pass the time. Sara teaches me an old hymn from Sunday school and I teach her *Hey Jude* and together we sing it out loud, keeping the silence at bay.

When I was a little girl my mum bought me a present, a forty-five single of *Hey Jude*. She adored the song, so did my brother, and so did I. We played it over and over again and danced up and down on our blue settees, each time the 'nah nah nahs' began. I liked the grooved black vinyl and the green apple on the record sleeve, and the small needle that stuck and jumped as we bounced. And as Sara and I sang out the song together across the silent Andes, the melody calmed my wrestless soul. I had found my lullaby at last.

CHAPTER FOUR

FOUND

MOUNT MOJANDA, ECUADOR, SOUTH AMERICA
12 DECEMBER 1998

A cloud veered across the blue sky like a random thought. I
followed its journey over the mountains as the rising sun cleared
the night of its stars. The air was filled with the scent of the earth
and the sound of waking birds. In the darkness every noise we
heard had led our imaginations to fatal scenarios. Falling leaves
were the sound of the rapists' footsteps returning and a rabbit
bolting was a killer in the bushes.

I followed the cloud as it changed shape like a dream and I
wondered where it would travel to and what it would turn into
next. It floated far away over the Andes, flying higher and growing
smaller, until it was just a tiny speck, like a white downy feather.

As it left my sight, something or someone had stepped into the periphery of my vision. We both ducked down into the ditch like wild animals, peering over the top of it. A woman had appeared behind us, dressed in light linen trousers and a woollen poncho. In her hands she carried a basket and waves of hay-coloured hair fell over her shoulders. Sara instantly heaved herself from her hiding place and ran over to the woman. I think she saw her as a saviour, but in my eyes she was a stranger, and strangers were deadly. Every single cell in my body was telling me not to trust her. Beneath her long hair and bohemian clothes, anyone could be hiding. I stayed in the ditch. My survival instinct was far stronger than my faith in human nature. Fight or flight – but I couldn't do either, so I stayed where I was and watched my friend approach the woman, praying that Sara wouldn't be attacked.

'We've been up the mountain all night. There were men there with guns!' cried Sara, blurting the words out as she ran towards the woman. As the stranger held her, Sara burst into tears and crumbled. The spell cast by the night had been lifted from her shoulders. She no longer had to be a leader, guiding us over stones through shards of moonlight and broken dreams. Finally she felt protected and could succumb to her fragility. We had been found. We were safe. We had been saved. I crawled out of the ditch and stumbled over to the woman who led us through a wooden gate and down a dirt track lane. But I didn't cry. I couldn't surrender to my vulnerability. I was far too fearful of her to let go.

'I'm Catherine,' she said, 'I live in the old farmhouse at the end of this lane.'

I think I can trust her, I thought to myself. She seems to be honest and earthy.

'You poor things, did they hurt you at all?'

'They held guns to our heads and two of them raped Isla,' Sara said.

The American woman looked at me solemnly, but I didn't say a word and neither were there any tears. Even though I'd defied death, I didn't feel the relief or joy of being alive. My thoughts returned to another time, some years ago, escaping from a fire, urgently kicking the glass from a window and crawling through the small gap I'd made to the safety of a ledge. I was carried down a ladder to the protection of strangers and huddled in an ambulance. I soon felt the euphoria of being alive, but on the peak of the mountain, I hadn't felt as though I'd cheated death – I knew that I'd faced evil. The men's faces, their smiles and laughter as they raped were now etched deep into my psyche.

Catherine opened the door of the farmhouse which led into a cluttered kitchen with an Aga in one corner. A small bundle of letters and a vase of wild flowers sat on top of a butcher's table, along with empty breakfast bowls waiting to be washed. Children's paintings were pinned onto the front of cupboard doors – blue trees, orange hills, and green, smiling suns. One of the pictures was signed by 'Dan' in bold, scrawling letters.

'How old's Dan?' Sara asked, smiling.

'Dan's six. He's the eldest, and then there's Grace, who's four, and baby Dominic – he's just turned two. They're all away for the day with my husband, thank God... Did I just say that out loud?' she laughed.

The American woman had children and fresh flowers; symbols of normality. She had made a home, a place where ordinary everyday events happened – school and day trips, breakfast plates, and a father. There weren't any trucks filled with men, or bleeding feet, or wind swirling through dark mountains. I felt I could trust her, and as my confidence in her grew, my survival instinct began to dissolve. The adrenalin, which had been surging around my body, was replaced with a natural morphine. Nature's way of coping with shock. It eased my aching body and calmed my mind, like a dreamy, hypnotic high. I stared at the small pink flowers in the cream curved vase, and specs of yellow pollen began to morph into grains of sand. I remembered this faraway feeling; it happened to me after the fire. I'd fallen into a distant state, completely removed from reality.

'Coffee?' asked the woman and she began to fill a glass cafetière with spoonfuls of ground, fresh grains. Its homely aroma filled the room, replacing the scent of trees, fauna, and cold night air which were still clinging to my clothes.

'Can I have a shower?' I asked.

'Of course – I'm sorry. I should have offered it straight away,' Catherine replied.

Quickly she led me upstairs into a large bathroom where the carpet was thick and felt soft. I stepped into a marble cubicle and turned on the jet, letting the water wash over me, soothing my weary body. The American had left some clothes out for me, folded on a blue wooden chair. The jumper and trousers were baggy and the cotton was soft. My own clothes were crumpled in my hands like yesterday's garbage. Slowly I walked down the carpeted stairs and sat at the table. Sara left to shower.

The coffee had been poured. A few ground grains clung to the inside of the mug, and like the pollen on the flowers they began to morph into specs of sand in front of me and my mind wandered to beaches, warm and soft like my clothes. A dream-like state enveloped me as I listened to the sound of the sea lapping at the shore.

'That mountain road is so dangerous. Only last week a group of tourists were held up there. No one was hurt but they got hold of everything valuable. I just can't believe the hostel didn't have a warning sign up. It's crazy that nobody told you.'

As I drank the coffee the granules gradually washed away from the side of the porcelain cup, like the sea claiming debris and driftwood. I felt the golden sand slipping through my fingers as the dream and the waves sang through my head. The American's words drifted over the lull of the ocean.

'Sorry, could you say that again?' I asked.

'Someone should have told you it was dangerous ... the road,' she repeated.

'So this kind of thing happens a lot?' I asked.

'Recently it has been,' she replied.

I sat in my dream, trying to make sense of what she was saying. 'What do you mean, exactly?' I asked.

Her words gradually began to have some meaning. 'It's been happening a lot in the past few weeks. I can't believe the police didn't warn all the hostels. Talking of which, I better go and call them. Are you going to be alright on your own for a second? The phone's in the other room.'

She made her way into the hallway. 'It's a shame nobody told you about that road,' she said as she left the room.

Her words were now coherent to me. A shame, she had said. A slight understatement, I'd thought. But I hadn't said it out loud. Any anger I felt had been dissipated by the morphine. My body was functioning well, doing what it was meant to do, calming my mind and veering it away from trauma, shock, and reality. I stared at a pattern of rings on the table, seams and wooden grooves, and I wondered which trees had made this table and where they had lived and what they had felt in their lifetime. My mind drifted into shady forests full of silence. It was menacing amongst the trees and I pulled my thoughts away from them, back to the present. But my reality was much more surreal and far, far darker.

The policeman arrived and stood in the kitchen surveying the room. His uniformed presence and the black large gun which swung from his belt felt intrusive amidst the mellow light and the children's naive paintings. He listened, and as Catherine explained the situation to him, talking in Spanish, he turned to look at me. There were no words of sympathy. Instead his stare seemed to ask, had I been pretty enough to rape? He turned away and I was left looking at the back of his light, blue shirt.

'He wants you both to go to the station later. Three in the afternoon – is that alright?' Catherine said.

'Okay,' I replied.

'And if you're ready, he'll give you a lift back to the hostel.'

Instinctively I asked the woman to come with us. The man before me held a gun.

CHAPTER FIVE

FOUND AGAIN

COVENT GARDEN, LONDON, ENGLAND

JANUARY 2002

January arrived, quietly making its presence known with the occasional blizzard of snow. The Exhibition Market was lifeless. Many of the traders had packed up their stalls for the month in search of sunnier climates. Empty spaces echoed between the aisles like gaping holes in a honeycomb, but Marcus's stall was open and today he'd appeared earlier than usual, bursting with smiles and generosity, buying rounds of tea for the traders. The reason behind his exuberant mood soon became apparent when Alexis, his brother, arrived. He'd been summoned by their mother to bail Marcus out of trouble. Like most stall holders at this time of year, Marcus's money belt was empty. Tourists were scarce and

Londoners were watching their pennies after the splurge of festive spending. But unlike other traders, Marcus hadn't saved for this bleak and quiet time. His love for Margaritas, made to perfection, and his desire for fine opium, bought at any price, meant that Marcus was usually a happy man, but more often than not a poor one. But he knew Alexis would always help him out, because unlike Marcus, his brother had a conscience.

Alexis was as successful in business as Marcus was not, and his advice to his brother had always been the same; there would never be any money found in lace toilet roll holders. But Marcus hated being told what to do and had remained loyal to his bathroom accessories. Although Alexis was cautious, and wore suits which were brown and rather predictable, his outlook on life was the same as his brother's, uplifting and drenched in bright orange. Before leaving he graciously presented Sal and me with a box of handmade chocolates, wrapped with yellow ribbon. Alexis didn't have Marcus's flamboyancy, but he certainly shared his charm.

By half past eleven the box was empty and as Big Ben chimed midday we unscrewed the top of a large bottle of vodka and poured out our first Bloody Mary. The ingredients of our sacred cocktail were kept in a box beneath my stall and guarded like the Holy Grail. As the concoction warmed our lips and raised our waning spirits, the boredom quickly melted like the newly fallen snow.

Though Sal delighted in our midday Marys, she seldom partook herself. 'You'll have livers like sponges,' she warned us both, but Marcus and I both agreed that tomorrow was another day and cirrhosis of the liver was more than a lifetime away.

Like two conspirators we poured out our drinks beneath the stall amongst patterned throws and yesterday's papers, taking great delight in our secret pastime. Very quickly the vodka had worked its magic and our freezing fingers, lips, noses, and toes began to thaw. Soon we were dancing in the aisles again like two frozen snowmen who had been brought back to life.

'The Sal is so boring ... she never has the drink,' Marcus declared, in a strong, Iranian accent as he spun me around Choi, a tall Singaporian man who sold plastic frogs and lizards which stuck to walls when thrown from a distance. I was both baffled and rather alarmed whenever he sold one.

'The Sal thinks she knows everything! This and that, this and that.'

This and that was a phrase Marcus often used when he couldn't be bothered to explain something. I liked the phrase. It was succinct, and I had begun to use it myself. He was also fond of using the prefix 'the' wherever he wanted, and Sal became 'The Sal', making Marcus, in my eyes, even more loveable. He quickly moved his thoughts away from The Sal and onto other more important topics, like the highs and lows of sex.

'If you have the sex, and it's good, you want it again and again,' he pontificated as he fondled his lace, 'but at the moment, as you know, I am single. So occasionally I have the one-night stand and then immediately I regret it. My mind is racing again, thinking about sex. I prefer, at the moment, for my thoughts to be at peace.' He gulped some more alcohol with relish and carried on philosophising, sitting upright on his tall chair like a modern day Bacchus. 'Of course, I would like the boyfriend, but it is so hard to find the right man. I don't like the faggot who is camp and acts like a queen, waving his hands around, speaking with the stupid voice. No, this is not for me. I like the man who looks straight and acts normal, without the camp ways. My ex – you've met him – he wasn't a faggoty queen.'

'So what went wrong?' I asked.

'I liked him at first, but in the end he was too normal and so boring, telling me off all the time. Do this and do that. No drugs, no drink ...' Marcus shook his head in disbelief. 'How can a person live like this?'

Ian, Marcus's ex, a kind and gentle man, was a senior nurse at Hammersmith Hospital. His temperament was the exact opposite of Marcus's: calm, measured, dutiful, and loyal. Sal called him dependable, but Marcus insisted that 'dependable' was the thin end of dull. It was obvious to all those around him that Ian was still in love with Marcus, and he often came to the market clutching a cheque, just like Marcus's brother, to help him out in his time of need.

Marcus leaned against his stall of lace tablecloths, toilet roll holders, and small furry teddy bears dressed in starch Beefeater jackets. Each tablecloth had a paper label pinned in one corner: Nottingham, handmade lace – £9.99.

Carlos, Marcus's Spanish friend, had bought them last month

at a street market in Nerja, a small town in southern Spain.

'Nerja, Nottingham, who cares? They begin with the same letter, don't they?' he said.

'Of course,' I agreed, 'they're both in the same continent. What more do people want for ten pounds?'

'Exactly! Some people expect the earth.'

And he turned the conversation away from the trivialities of his livelihood to more pressing concerns, such as the nature of love. Currently Carlos, the young tablecloth smuggler, was in the process of breaking Marcus's heart.

'He is straight, so he says, but he teases me, Isla. He teases me.'

'In what way?' I asked, enthralled.

'We go out to the club until four. He stays in my bed, but nothing happens. Not a kiss ... nothing. Maybe the occasional cuddle, but that's all. Nothing else. For weeks this has been going on, and now he is here in my head.' Marcus tapped his forehead to emphasise exactly where Carlos had bored into.

'I suppose you've tried not seeing him for a while?' I suggested.

'Of course I've tried, but all the time I think about him. In the morning I make the coffee, I put the sugar in, I stir with the spoon, and it clinks on the side. Round and round, clink, clink, clink ... and before I know it, the coffee's gone cold, the clock has ticked by, and my thoughts have been lost ... all on him. Why do you think I'm always so late for work?' he laughed.

I understood exactly why Marcus had an obsession with Spanish Carlos. He was indisputably beautiful with dark brown eyes like a Romany's and the aura of a cherub. The mixture of a rugged Heathcliffe combined with shades of innocence was a winning combination.

'He's like a work of art,' I'd once said to Sal.

'He's a cocky little upstart,' she had replied.

But Marcus and I were romantics, and as we sipped our Bloody Marys, watching the occasional customer step through the aisles, avoiding the snow, he began to soliloquise about the joys and tragedies which befell such romantic souls as ours.

'I imagine that you are like me in matters of the heart,' he said. 'When we fall in love, Isla, we fall very deeply. It lifts us to a higher place ... up, up, up ... higher than the Big Ben, higher than the aeroplane. Even the drugs cannot reach this place. But what goes up must come down. That is the law? Yes? And it hurts so much to fall from such a height. If our hearts break it splits us in two. We crumble like the ruin until we fade to dust. And there are some people where the heart stays forever in two ... nothing can repair it. And so when love comes in sight again, knocking at the door, they dare not take a chance. To lose once more is too much to bear, and so the romantic soul becomes the most solitary of all. They refuse to risk any more pain and so they stay by themselves, and their closest partner is loneliness. The Spanish boy is dangerous. I am beginning to fall in love again, and I don't think I want to.'

Marcus sprinkled more pepper into his drink, as if to emphasise the heat of the situation.

'It is often people like The Sal who have the easiest times. The life, to her, is black and white. They seldom fall in love so deeply, and so they have less to lose.'

I drank some more Bloody Mary and played thoughtfully with a toilet roll holder. 'Marcus,' I said, 'you're talking to a romantic so I can't really advise you. I'm the same creature as you. If you want some sound, practical advice then I think you should talk to Sal.'

'No, not The Sal. Business, yes. Love, no.'

Marcus carried on with his lover's lament. 'I first fell in love when I was eighteen years old. He was an older man. Good looking, wealthy, in control. But young at heart and in the bedroom ... you know?' Marcus smiled wistfully. 'I followed him all over the world using money my father gave me in his will. He died when I was seventeen and left me a small fortune. In Iran it is the tradition to give the youngest of the children the money, and I am the baby of the family so I had his wealth. Thankfully he died before the revolution took it all.'

'What do you mean, took it all?' I asked, intrigued by Marcus's previous life.

'We were very rich – aristocracy – but the Ayotollah came and took everything we owned. We fled for our lives and lived in the mountains, eating berries and nuts for month after month.'

'Really?' I was amazed.

'Of course. I am not the commoner like The Sal and these people around me. I was rich and lived like the king, and now look at me!' Marcus sighed. 'Anyway, I spent my father's money on meeting my lover in glorious cities all over the world. But my situation with this man was impossible, like life often is. He was married, you see? With a child.'

And Marcus told me the tale of his first broken heart, of clandestine meetings with his businessman lover in hotels and apartments all over the globe. But the excitement eventually turned sour and after two years of yearning, Marcus knew that the person he adored would never leave his wife, and all he could hope for was a lifetime of being 'the other man'. So finally he turned his back on the doomed affair and set to work on finding other more healthy distractions.

'I turned to roulette,' he said and laughed at his own irreverent nature. Marcus sighed heavily and drank the last drops of his Bloody Mary. 'Oh, Isla. The faggot life ... it's the hardest life of all ... I cannot sit with the men like Nouri and his brother and talk about football and have the pint and the fish and the chip.'

Nouri was the only other Iranian at The Exhibition Market. He was a large, kind man who made a small fortune selling calendars of Hollywood Hunks to swooning girls and occasionally to Marcus. Twice a year he tried to increase his small fortune to a large one and flew to Las Vegas with his Polish brother-in-law. Sometimes he was lucky, and occasionally he was not. The fortunate times were rehashed with exuberance on his return as Nouri flitted in and out of the stalls with tales of magic aces and five-card tricks. The unluckier times were never mentioned, but Nouri's pursed lips spoke volumes.

'Yet, as much as I cannot sit with the man, I cannot sit with the woman either and listen to their gossip. He said, she said, he said, she said. It bores me ... the faggot life is such a hard life.' And suddenly Marcus looked older than his years and his beautiful brown eyes filled with melancholy like a man who'd spent too long at sea. 'The faggot life is the life of the outsider,' he sighed, 'do you know how that feels?'

'I do,' I said. And as I sat next to this charming outsider, I felt a unique bond with him, for I was an outcast too. I was a raped girl. The residue of sorrow and the aftermath of violation had left me feeling different from those around me, alienating me from the rest of society. I didn't belong anywhere anymore and my ties to the rest of civilization had melted away, as though I'd been standing on a frozen lake, watching the ice gradually thaw around me. I could no longer get back to the shore. There wasn't a way home. In my mind's eye I could picture different pockets of humanity standing on the shoreline, but I could barely recognise them anymore. I had no one to relate to. I could make out the outline of a mother with her children pulling at her dress and I could see people hurtling through their careers. I also glimpsed those who lived cosily in country cottages with dogs and warmth and wooden furniture, and waving to me on the water's edge were actors and musicians, playfully trying on costumes, preening and laughing, fawning and chatting, drinking in their lust for life. But it all meant nothing to me, for I was far away from them all now.

I was a raped girl who could no longer reach them.

But Marcus had thrown me a lifeline and had reeled me in with his ribbons of lace. With his past of broken hearts, harboured sorrows, and a profound sense of experiencing life as an outsider, I had found someone I could relate to – a long-lost brother, a kindred spirit. Finally there was someone to communicate with on the shore, or maybe Marcus had joined me on my solitary ice patch, but together we'd found our own territory in the unlikeliest of places, amongst traders and tourists, tittle and tat.

'Come. Let's go see how another faggot life is going. I'm tired of mine. Come. Let's go see Gabriel.'

Gabriel, just like the paintings he sold, added a colourful dimension to the market. He was a bronzed Brazilian, tall and manly with short fluffy hair and wide smiling eyes like a tumble-dried teddy bear. Emblazoned on his right arm was a tattoo of an eagle, the colour of May skies, but unfortunately in winter his taut biceps were covered by layers of jumpers, much to the disappointment of the female fraternity.

Gabriel lit a cigarette and the smoke swirled through the aisles and up into the rafters where the pigeons were perched, huddled together in a bid to keep warm. He began to rehash his previous night's adventures; dining in Soho, drinking in Mayfair, and dancing in Vauxhall. He clearly remembered the sun coming up but had no recollection of how he'd got home. By the time he'd risen in the morning, night buses, mini cabs, and the first tube at dawn had all faded from his memory. The whens and the hows still slept on his pillow where last night's lover's head now lay.

'I hope he is still there when I get home,' Gabriel said. 'He can sleep all day like a baby, as far as I care, as long as he's a man when I open the door.' Gabriel winked and gave me a look which made me wish I was a gay man, and more specifically, the man who was in Gabriel's bed. I left the two friends talking and took my pew behind my stall, replacing the highs of the vodka for an earthy cup of tea before escaping into the pages of a book which Carl, my reckless friend, had given me.

Carl was gaunt, good looking, strangely manic, and worked part-time for Will, my boss, in his warehouse. He was also an occasional drug dealer, and more often than not, an intellectual pontificator. Reading was his passion, and as soon as he'd devoured a book he passed it straight on to me. I picked up his latest offering, nestled next to the vodka in the Holy Grail box, beneath the shrouded stall.

Milan Kundera: *The Unbearable Lightness of Being*

I wasn't entirely sure how the atmosphere of fast-talking traders would be conducive to absorbing melancholy thoughts on the human condition, yet with the aisles as empty as the Arctic and the vodka tucked away until mid-afternoon, there was nothing else to distract me from my own mind, so I opened the book and prepared to spend an afternoon in a world of existential angst. However, I'd barely finished the first chapter before Marcus reappeared, bearing the look of an anguished man, even more so than Kundera himself, and snatched the book from out of my hands, whisking it back to his stall. Immediately I joined him at his lace to discover the cause of such pain.

'The Spanish boy is coming! He text me just now!' Marcus repeatedly tapped the screen of his phone, emphasising the urgency. 'When he arrives I want to be reading the book, like this ...'

He opened the book and looked at the pages intensely. 'What do you think? Do you think I look intelligent? I want him to see that even though I may be an older man, I am a clever man. Someone he can look up to and admire, someone who has lived a life, a person with intelligence, and not just some bald faggot working at the market. I want to talk in an educated way about this book. What is it about?'

'The burden of morality, soullessness, tyranny, despair ...'

'Okay, maybe I won't. But I look good, eh?'

'Yes. You look very knowledgeable,' I said.

'Good, good. Go, go!' he said urgently, 'I have to look like I've been reading this for hours.'

I left Marcus at his stall and crossed over the aisles to Sal's tea shop with its shelves festooned with tea caddies and brightly coloured china. There was a new product for sale: teabags from India which promised to soothe all those who were world-weary and worn.

Behind her counter was a small wrought iron radiator, but the way we revered it for its life-giving heat, it could have been made from pure gold. We sat with our legs facing the warmth, huddled together like the pigeons in the rafters above. The afternoon grew even colder and Marcus and Carlos' voices drifted across the market, blown by the wind, the occasional word hitting us like raindrops.

'If I hear one more blast of false laughter, I'll go over and shut Marcus up myself!' Sal said. 'Talk about making it obvious ... Has he no bloody shame?'

But Marcus was on a different plane, and the usually small amount of logic a romantic soul does possess had left him a long time before. Love had hit him hard. Like a euphoric high, like the warm surge of alcohol running through the veins, like the tumultuous wind rushing over the Moors. Marcus was lost in his own private world.

The laughter continued and Carlos stayed with him the whole of the afternoon. Marcus bought him a Thai lunch, which they ate at the stall from small cardboard boxes, and later he treated them to afternoon cakes from an exquisite patisserie, as old as the Normandy hills. Together they devoured a box of almond cakes, glazed and topped with icing sugar.

'Bloody hell! The almond cakes have arrived. He must be in love! He only ever gives them to mugs who'll lend him money,' Sal exclaimed.

At the end of the day, when the sky was dark by four o'clock, Marcus closed the shutters on his toilet roll emporium, and he and Carlos left together. The almond cakes had worked their magic. As a last thought, before leaving Marcus popped Kundera into his bag and gave me a farewell wink, charm exuding from him like rays of invisible sun.

'Bless him,' Sal said and she shook her head despairingly. She had no doubt in her mind that the love affair was hopeless and Marcus's heart would be crushed into smithereens and left scattered in the aisles. 'And it'll be you and me who have to pick up the pieces – just you wait. Spanishy's using him,' Sal said, 'free clubs, free dinners, and free bloody almond cakes. This ain't gonna end well. Mark my words.'

And with her parting piece of rhetoric, she pulled down the metal shutters of her small, cosy shop. The dramas of the day had come to a close. 'Ta ta,' she said and made her way through the aisles towards her home overlooking Leather Lane Market and lifetimes of history.

Before making my own way home, I walked past the underground to the banks of The Thames, enchanted by the fairy lights across the water swaying in the branches of the bare winter trees. As I walked over the narrow footbridge, a light sprinkling of snow began to fall onto the commuters' macs, hats, and shiny shoes as they hurried back to the warmth of their homes. With the fairy lights beckoning and the snowflakes falling, I felt like I was crossing over into Narnia, travelling onwards to an unknown adventure, and I thought about my childhood room and the mouse that ticked and tocked by the side of the bed while I turned over the pages of an old, worn book. And finally, in this cold, dark month of January, after months of carrying the weight of sorrow,

I'd found enchantment again. Yet the treasure wasn't hidden through the back of a wardrobe, but behind the stalls of a market, where a beautiful bald man pontificated about love and life was stranger than fiction.

A small, narrow boat passed beneath the bridge. Its hub was dark green. The driver waved up at us, his smile just visible over the top of his scarf. As he chugged through the water, like a drifting Poohstick, he didn't appear worried by the white icy flakes falling around him, and I wondered where he was going. Maybe even he didn't know, and that was why he looked so happy, the joy of seeing where the river might take him.

CHAPTER SIX
NO MAN'S LAND

OTOVALO, ECUADOR, SOUTH AMERICA
14 DECEMBER 1998

That night we slept in the dormitory, instead of our private room, preferring the presence of people. All the bunks were taken so we pulled the mattress from our bed, heaved it across the courtyard and over a patch of grass where two goats were grazing and chickens pecked and clucked. This was my first night back in the hostel since I'd been raped and I didn't want to sleep alone. I had visions of the rapists striding into the police station, demanding to know where we were staying, tracking us down like wild animals in a bid to keep our mouths shut forever. I could hear the clatter of breaking glass as they shattered the windows of our room and the sound of our screams as they gagged us again, forcing the cold metal of their guns to our heads. Andréa assured me this wouldn't happen, but I couldn't take her words for granted. It would be difficult to take anything for granted again.

We put the mattress into the middle of the dormitory, making sure we were totally surrounded by the other girls. I could tell by their occasional glances and sideways stares that they knew about our nightmare, but no one said a word. For this I was grateful; I appreciated their distance. Awkward consolations or gossip disguised as concern would have only added to our anxiety. The ordeal was over, and it was time to sleep. I thought about the sleeping tablets the doctor had prescribed me and found them stuffed into my woollen cardigan's pocket in a silver packet. Doctor Merusio, a little, lean man, had arrived that afternoon at the hostel to examine me. Dressed in a brown old-fashioned suit with a matching trilby and tortoise-shell glasses, his English was like poetry, soulful and melancholy. He parted with a final comment: 'I am so sorry this happened to you – I apologise for my country.'

Here, stood before me was a professional man who had studied hard and worked diligently to serve a community, yet his government was corrupt, his country was poor, and he was powerless to change it. Instead he consoled me with sleeping tablets and Valium, wrapping them in tissue and placing them on top of the bedside dresser before closing the door behind him. That night I vowed to sleep without his drugs. If I could find sleep naturally, it would mean the rapists hadn't won. It would signify that I still had the peace of mind to fall into slumber – they hadn't destroyed the whole of me.

During the night the clouds came and scattered rain over the mountains. The morning grass was lush and wet and the rubble courtyard had lost its dust. Cool air blew from the Andes while the chickens hid in their coops. I had managed to sleep through the night and found some comfort in that. Now it was time to endure another day. I grabbed my blue towel, drying on the radiator from the night before, and stumbled into the shower room. A girl in her early twenties with red platted hair came out of the cubicle and smiled at me sympathetically. I was now a victim, someone to feel sorry for, and I hated it. Her reaction was kind, but it robbed me of my pride. I acknowledged her briefly and stepped into the shower.

Half an hour later I found Sara in the common room where breakfast was served in the morning to travellers who told tales over beers through the night. The room was warm and cosy, its clean white walls adorned with soft woollen rugs. There was an open log fire in the middle of the room. It was here, three days ago, that Sara and I first heard about the Mojanda Lakes from an animated Dutch girl who'd been up the mountain that day and had vividly described the beautiful views from the top. It was well worth the hike, she'd told us. I remember the girl clearly as she and I ended the night impersonating pigs, 'oinking' in the bar with beers in our hands and grins on our faces. Her face is etched deep in my memory. This girl had inadvertently led us up the mountain with her innocent recommendation – our chance conversation had changed my life.

'Hi,' I said to Sara and sat down next to her.

She was sitting by the fire, prodding the embers.

'I couldn't sleep,' Sara said, 'All I could think of is us walking all the way down that mountain without any shoes. It makes me feel so sad. I've been sitting by this fire all night.'

Sara hadn't slept at all and had found her way to the bar in the early hours of the morning. Robin, the young Australian barman, had still been awake and while Sara poured out her sadness, Robin had served out the drinks.

'Why don't you try and get some sleep?' I suggested. 'The dorms are empty now – it'll be quiet in there. I'll wake you at two.'

We had to be at the police station at three to collect our passports; the police had kept them for bureaucratic reasons. Sara left, weary and small.

'Sounds like you too really went through it,' said Robin. 'Sara was saying how petrified she'd been when the guns came out.'

Unlike Sara, I couldn't talk about the experience, and I wondered if that was because Sara hadn't been raped. The attack had destroyed me. Every positive quality I'd learned as a child – goodness, kindness, warmth, and love – were key to my outlook on life, but now I had witnessed evil. My world was now a place where men forced women to have sex with them and laughed at their own brutality. The rapists had brought darkness into my consciousness and opened the door to an alternative world that I had never before entered. Child abuse, paedophilia, murder, rape, torture, abductions – all these crimes were no longer just headlines in a newspaper; they were intensely real. The cruelty of the world and its sorrow seeped into me, making me vulnerable, making me sad. All the good in the world had been overshadowed by darkness and my trust in human nature was gone. It was impossible to explain this to Robin. He was a young traveller on an adventure – not a therapist – so I spared us both any awkwardness and took a book over to the fireside and began to read. I was determined to get through at least one chapter, even though my concentration was shot. If I could absorb the words, I would score another victory – just like sleeping without the sleeping tablets – it would show to me that I still had some peace of mind and that the rapists hadn't won.

Sara woke earlier than two and joined me in the courtyard where I sat on a hand-woven blanket, shielding my eyes from the sun which had found a way through the clouds.

'Are you okay?' I asked.

'Yes, I slept well. I feel a lot better – do you?'

Better than what, I thought. Better than being sat in a dark room relating a rape story to a belligerent policeman? Better than walking down a mountain with bleeding feet? Yes, I had to admit I did feel better, when I looked at it that way.

'I suppose I do,' I replied.

Sara suggested we bathe our feet again before going to the police station, and she went and fetched some hot water. A childlike innocence came over her as she burst the blisters, like popping bubble wrap. She found something immensely satisfying in it and began to laugh. Her laughter lightened the atmosphere and we began to speak more freely.

'The worst thing of all, 'Sara said, 'was the way the men just popped up from out of nowhere.' At this point, I began to giggle. 'What's funny?' she asked.

'Popped up? Popping up is what toast does – it pops up from the toaster. Three men with guns don't pop up.'

We burst into fits of laughter. The understatement had been intentional and that was something I loved about Sara – her irreverent sense of humour. It was our shared sense of the ridiculous and our curious natures that had bound us together as friends. I first heard about Sara from Ryan, a friend of mine from school, who'd met her in his first few weeks at university. Day in and day out he'd talked non-stop about a pretty, witty, hippy girl who'd totally entranced him. Eventually, I was allowed to meet her and we hit it off immediately, exploring the sights and sounds of London together from squat parties in Brixton, to picnics on the Vale of the Heath. Sara graduated as a speech therapist and began to work in a hospital, but after three years the workload and London had begun to take its toll. She needed some time away and that's what had led us to South America. Sara wanted an adventure and I'd been a willing companion, so we each bought a six-month open ticket which began with a flight to Ecuador.

Robin brought out two mugs of coffee, on the house, and placed them next to the blanket on a smooth paving stone. His actions were gentle and hesitant, as if they portrayed his thoughts. We drank the coffee, dried our feet, and sat a while longer in the sun. The caffeine revived us in time for our journey back to the police station, and as it neared three o'clock, we jumped in the car with Fabio, Andréa's husband, and drove five kilometres downhill into Otovalo. Fabio, like his wife, was full of gusto and joked about the locals along the way but as we neared Otovalo he suddenly became serious, his arms stopped gesticulating, and he sat up straight.

'Alert your eyes for the blue pick-up truck,' Fabio instructed.

'What blue pick-up truck?' I asked.

'The truck those bastards were driving.' He looked at me in the back of the car through his rear-view mirror. I looked back at him blankly. 'The arseholes on the mountain,' he said.

'You think they might be here, in the town?' I was shocked.

'Of course. There's no other town for twenty kilometres. They may even live here.'

It hadn't occurred to me they could live here. It hadn't occurred to me they might live anywhere. The thought of them in their homes gave the rapists another dimension; it elevated them from random feral sociopaths to real human beings who took part in everyday life. Who cooked or were cooked for, who listened to music or maybe even played it, who watched TV, and slept in beds and stretched and dreamed. I began to wonder who else might live in their homes and whom they went home to the night they raped me – a mother, a sister, a wife, or a lover? Did they look into that woman's eyes and think, 'Today I did a terrible thing', or had they raped so many times that they no longer had a conscience?

'We can ride around for a while – go to the villages – see if we can find it?' Fabio suggested.

'Could you do me a favour?' I asked him. 'Can you come back and look for it while I'm not here?'

'Of course,' he agreed, 'let's get to the station.'

There were no police cars outside the station when we got there, and no lights shining through the window. We banged on the door, and the building was empty. Stepping over tyres and parts of disused engines, we made our way around to the back and looked through the windows of the interview rooms. Both of them were deserted; the station was closed. Sara searched in her bag for something to write on and found a leaflet at the bottom for a Christmas Day Feast in the Paulo Tavern, the restaurant where we'd eaten on our first night in town. The bus had dropped us off next to the small town square. All the streets were empty and the only light had come from the stars and one solitary street lamp next to a bench. A sign swung from a building half way down a side street and a warm glow shone from its windows, reflecting a dreamy amber light onto the road. We'd followed the glow and found ourselves in a homely pizzeria.

Sara wrote on the back of the flyer and put it through the letter box.

'WE NEED OUR PASSPORTS BACK. WHEN YOU GET IN CALL US ON X. WE'RE AT THE FINO FLARE HOSTEL.'

When we got back to the hostel we began a period of waiting, a time of timelessness. Like stepping into no-man's-land, time didn't belong to anyone or anywhere; it just simply passed, and each day became like the last. Every morning we ate our breakfast at wooden block tables and drank strong, thick coffee, like Turkish coffee, poured into bowls as the French do. Afterwards we'd drive into town, passing farmers and the occasional llama, only to find the police station shut. Each evening we sat by the fire, playing cards, chatting aimlessly, and reading books. Inside I was hollow and numb, but I followed Sara's lead.

On one of the afternoons of waiting, we made the decision to call our boyfriends. They were flying out to meet us in less than a week. We'd all booked our tickets at the same time, trawling the internet, eager for bargains. It was time to break the news to them and the prospect of the phone call began to make me anxious. The phone was in Andréa's office. I stepped inside and sat down at the desk. The room felt relaxed. It wasn't an anal office based on precision. It felt more like a home – someone's private universe, with photos pinned to a notice board and sketches scribbled on pads. I doubted whether anyone could base their lives on precision in Ecuador. The only way to live in this country was to take life as you found it. I lit a cigarette and thought about Ollie. Ollie was upbeat and fun and our relationship was similar, but that's where it ended. Together we hadn't reached a point where we'd gained a deeper awareness of each other or a natural understanding that usually comes with time. I needed to speak to someone who had insight into my mind; someone I could connect to. I had close friends who were like family. We shared a history of over fifteen years and our understanding of each other ran deep. I should have called them, but I had to tell Ollie. Deep down, all I wanted to do was call my parents and ask them to fly to Ecuador and take me back to the family home where I'd be safe and warm, cared for and loved. I picked up the phone and dialled my parents' number but immediately hung up. I had visions of my mum speaking softly into the receiver, gentle in her ways, kindly asking how I was and the phone slipping from her hand as I told her my news, her face contorting with tears and fear sweeping through her. Her daughter was three thousand miles away in a town where three men who'd raped her could be living round the corner. I couldn't find the will to make the call or the heart to break theirs. I dialled Ollie's number, and it rang out. I knew when he answered there would be some kind of scene occurring, and if there wasn't he would quickly create one. Ollie was an actor and his love of drama filtered through into his everyday life. He was fascinated by the smallest nuances of the world and as intrigued by the contents listed on a chocolate bar wrapper as most people were by the British Museum. His humour, like Sara's, was irreverent and surreal. On the sixth ring he answered and the drama began.

'Hi – I'm on a bus in Notting Hill, on my way to Darren's. It's really busy and Christmassy outside. There's an old grey-haired man sitting at the front, eating a pretzel, and a young man sitting next to him with a bag of chips ...'

'Ollie, I've got something to tell you.'

'... and the pretzel man said to the chips man, "Put your chips away – they stink!" The chips man was furious and said, "Hey old man ..."'

'Ollie, listen to me. I've got something to tell you.'

'"... don't diss me, sat there with your pretzel ..."'

'Stop and listen!'

'Sorry, sorry ... what is it you've got to tell me?'

'Me and Sara went up a mountain – we were attacked. They raped me.'

'They? Who the fuck are they?'

'There were three of them on the mountain with guns – two of them raped me.'

There was a long silence and I could hear the bustle of London in the background. I suddenly longed to be on the bus, sat next to Ollie, whispering about the pretzel man and making up his life.

'Come back! Fly back as soon as you can,' Ollie insisted.

'I can't come back. I haven't got my passport.'

'Where is it?'

'At the police station – but the police aren't there.'

'Where are they?'

'I don't know. They've disappeared. We've been back four times.'

'If they're not there tomorrow, call the British Consulate and then call me – okay?'

'Okay.'

'Isla, listen. Stay exactly where you are. I'll call you when I get to Darren's.'

When Ali, Sara's boyfriend, called her back he was crying. He'd spent the past hour punching cushions, hitting furniture, and venting his fury on various objects, hurling them around the room. I thought this was a normal reaction; his feelings of anger had to be released somehow. But when Ollie called back he was calm, lucid, and in control, and his reaction seemed almost incredible. It was as though I'd told him I'd slipped on the mountain and had broken an arm. His flippancy hurt me and I could only deduce from our conversation that he didn't really care. Five years later his flatmate, who was living with him at the time, told me that Ollie came home that night and had cried inconsolably, but this news came five years too late – I needed to know at the time. His empathy would have been a lifeline for me but Ollie had masked his real feelings behind an image of what he thought a man ought to be. But Ollie wasn't a real-men-don't-cry kind of person and I'd never known him as one. He left me feeling bewildered. A thread of misunderstanding had begun to weave its way into our relationship, like termites weakening wood.

That evening Sara and I sat at the block tables and ate a bowl of pollo sin pollo, a traditional Ecuadorian stew, and drank a few beers by the fire. The evenings were like Britain in the spring, and once the sun had left the sky, the air cooled rapidly. We'd watched the sun set every evening, filling the sky with shades of pink, red, and lilac, like watercolour paints dripping through the sky. One night Sara broke the silence of our faraway stares by recounting a conversation she'd had with Ali that day.

'Ali said we both went through an extremely terrifying ordeal,' said Sara.

I wasn't entirely sure why she said this as it seemed to be stating the obvious.

'Of course we did,' I said, 'we both know that.'

'But he said it had been terrifying for us both,' she said, emphasising the word 'both'.

'Me as well as you.' I still wasn't sure where this conversation was leading. 'I know – we know – we were both terrified,' I said.

'I think what Ali was trying to say was that we went through the same thing.'

Her words made me instantly defensive. 'But we didn't. We didn't go through the same thing,' I said.

'Not exactly, but we were both really scared and thought we might die.'

'Yes. But we didn't go through the same thing.'

'I know, but it was very scary for us both. That's all,' Sara concluded.

I wasn't convinced I knew exactly what Sara was trying to say, but the connotation of her conversation with Ali made me feel uncomfortable. I mulled over her words, dealing out the cards – black on red, queen on king – and I realised since we'd given our statements that Sara hadn't talked about the rapes, as if they hadn't happened. Both Ollie and Sara seemed to be ignoring an act of incredible violence and I began to feel alienated. It was as though middle England had suddenly arrived at the hotel and had whispered in Sara's ear: Let's not bring any more attention to this – brush it all under the carpet – rape really is a social taboo, so what would people think, making such a fuss? Perhaps Sara and Ali really did think gang rape was of no consequence but Sara was a woman, and rape is predominantly a crime against females – every woman's nightmare. I expected her to unite with me, not only as a friend but as an act of sisterhood. The rapes were not only a violation against me, but the ultimate disrespect to all of womankind. My body had been used for another person's gain, like slavery. Slavery was abolished in 1833, but rape was still common. It was not only right here, right now in this room where we sat, but all over the world. At the same time as I was dealing out the cards, women were being raped, domestically abused, violated in their own homes, having their clitorises burned from their bodies – all acts of disempowerment and violence carried out by men. Rape was so atrocious, I'd taken it for granted that Sara would feel the same way about it, yet here she was turning her back on her fellow woman. Sara wasn't holding out the hand of solidarity. Instead it seemed she was joining with Ali as a force against me. I thought we were both sailing in the same boat, battling through this hurricane as best as we could together, but now Sara had forged a wedge between us and had made our plight her own. I rummaged through my mind for reasons and could only come to the conclusion that Sara needed Ali to know how much she was suffering and saw me as a threat; somebody who might take away the attention she both wanted and deserved.

I was too exhausted to question her or confront her, so I left the room instead, leaving the friction behind me. Both Sara and I were in pain. There was not going to be an easy way through this. I grabbed my towel from the dormitory and stumbled into the bathroom, hoping a warm shower would wash away my stress. Turning the silver dial to hot, I leaned against the tiled wall. My body relaxed beneath the water and I slid down the tiles and sat in the corner of the cubicle. Resting my head on my knees, I cried.

The following morning we arrived at the police station, only to find it shut. Later in the day I called the British Consulate. The word rape hadn't stopped the breezy receptionist's flow, but the young man she put me through to was filled with concern.

'Miss Nutbrown?'

'Yes, hi.'

'Hi. I understand you were …' – he struggled to find the appropriate word – '… attacked.' He concluded.

'Yes, I was raped.'

'I'm sorry to hear that –'

I cut him short. I was tired and my nerves were raw. I didn't have the patience to speak more than necessary. 'We can't get out of Otovalo. We want to leave but –'

It was his turn to be abrupt. 'Miss Nutbrown. First, I have to say, this is a matter of extreme emergency. You must come to the Consulate as soon as possible.'

'We can't. Our passports are with the police in the police

station, but the station's been shut since we left them there.'

'When was that?' he asked.

'Three … four days ago.'

'There's a strong possibility the police have taken them and sold them on by now. I'm going to have to get someone higher up to intervene immediately.' He wrote down some details – police, dates, and times. 'You must come here as soon as possible. Can either of you drive?'

Neither of us held a licence.

'Do you have friends who can bring you?'

'No. We came alone.'

'Perhaps you can get a taxi?'

I refused to get into a taxi. I had strong doubts about the taxi driver who'd driven us up the mountain – he could have been the one who told the rapists of our whereabouts. They could have been his friends. Two women alone, good cameras, nice shoes … I couldn't trust taxis.

'We'll get a bus,' I said. 'Do you know when they are?'

He checked his information quickly. 'There's one at seven this evening, arriving in Quito at ten past midnight. I really do suggest you get this bus if you can and come and see us in the morning. This is an emergency – it needs to be dealt with urgently.'

At last somebody seemed to be taking me seriously. The man had eased my mind. Rape was an emergency, and I wasn't being melodramatic.

'Thanks,' I said, 'we'll try and get there tonight.'

'Just get here as soon as you can. Take care.'

As the man hung up I imagined him in his warm, safe office, pulling on his jacket at the end of the day and stepping out into the city, walking through streets lined with bars and restaurants and stopping for a few after-work drinks, chatting and laughing with colleagues and friends. I longed for the anonymity of the city again, to be amongst civilization and life and to leave behind the mountains and their ominous silence, except for the sound of the wind bending the corn as it made its way to the sea.

That night we finally left Otovalo. The bus arrived an hour late, rickety and worn with painted orange panels, like a big VW camper van. An old man carrying bags in his hands and weariness on his face, was the only other passenger travelling from Otovalo. At Cotachi, the next village on, two loud middle-aged men boarded the bus and stood by the driver, chatting openly and freely with him like long-lost friends. Not long after they boarded they cracked open a large bottle of whiskey, and the bus driver joined in, grabbing a bottle from beneath his seat, gulping away as happy as a baby at a bottle. As time went by their laughter increased and their voices grew louder. The driver was drunk. The mountain road was narrow and the bus veered around the bends as precariously as a ballerina on a tightrope. Every now and then I dared to look out of the window only to see sheer drops, crumbling roads, and the occasional burned-out vehicle crushed at the bottom of the mountainside. I averted my eyes away from the road, looked up at the stars, and wondered to myself what on earth had happened.

What cosmic force had picked me up and catapulted me into this reality, changing my life forever? Two weeks ago I'd been filming *Casualty*, dancing in a basement nightclub in Bristol with Charlie Fairhead, a national treasure, laughing with the crew, joking with the actors, happy with my life, and secure in my future. Now, here I was, my soul destroyed, my passport stolen, sitting on a bus with a drunk bus driver who was merrily juggling with a wheel, a whiskey bottle, and my life. Even the storyline of *Casualty* was more plausible than this, I thought, and dragged my rucksack down from the rack above me and got out my book, trying to take my mind away from the bus driver and his penchant for booze. After everything we'd been through, were we going to die on a bus? I'd know soon enough, I thought to myself, and surrendered myself to fate.

CHAPTER SEVEN

THE SAL

COVENT GARDEN, LONDON, ENGLAND

AUGUST 2002

I threw open the door of my small terraced flat and stepped out onto the pavement. Aislop Road was bathed in a lemon sun, enhancing the street with a friendly feel and warming my bare arms and face. I was fifteen minutes late. Quickly I locked the red door behind me and began to run towards the bus stop, halting at the busy Mile End Road, waiting for a lull in the traffic. It was Thursday, dustbin day, and large, loud refuge lorries crawled along the high street, cluttering the road, filling the city with dust. A van pulled up next to a small corner shop and the driver began to heave out its contents, tins of pet food stacked into boxes and bottles of milk chiming in crates. Suddenly I was aware I'd forgotten to feed

Suli, my cat. My conscience got the better of me and I hurtled back down the street, sprang through the door, spooned some tuna into Her Highness' dish and ran back to the bus stop, weaving my way through the lorries again. The red double-decker stopped dutifully at the shelter and the passengers jumped on, gathering around the stairwell, fumbling their way up the narrow staircase, before sitting down on the fuzzy-feeling seats. Sitting in front of me were a young couple dressed stylishly in retro clothing. The short-bobbed girl was staring out of the window, defiantly ignoring her boyfriend who was begging her to talk to him. Sitting a few seats behind was a group of teenagers firing off nicknames and sharing sought-after secrets.

The bus weaved its way through Bethnal Green, chugging past the grey-bricked Buddhist centre and glass-fronted health food stores, before turning left into Shoreditch High Street where neon bars with pool tables served pitchers of beer and a New York sensation. Further up the high street, as the bus made its way towards the city the bars were replaced by offices, housed in majestic glass buildings, reflecting the sun like fountains cascading in the sky. I glanced at my watch again. I was now over half an hour late, but the morning was so beautiful, with its egg blue sky and golden sun that my thoughts drifted off into the clouds, and time and lateness ceased to exist. The phone in my bag began to buzz. It was Sal, bringing me back down to earth with a text.

'Where are you, madam? Are you out of bed yet? It's nearly half past ten!'

I could picture her standing outside her small market shop, saying her hellos and good mornings, and drinking tea before whisking herself over to Deborah and Tony's stall to catch up on any gossip. Sal was fascinated by Deborah and Tony's love life, as was I and nearly the whole of the market. Tony, a softly spoken Londoner, had employed Deborah to work for him twenty years ago. Deborah had been a young witty twenty-one-year-old back then, with strawberry blond hair and long dancer's legs, and even though Tony was twice her age, they'd soon fallen in love. But Tony was married, and still is to this day, with children and grandchildren, cats, and a dog. Whether Deborah is content, no one really knows, because as Deborah knows so well, all market stalls have ears. To this day she has remained tactfully silent. They used to sell records, but now they stock cds, and in all their twenty years of trading, the musical format is the only thing that's changed.

I imagined Sal and Deborah laughing together about my lackadaisical ways and dislike of early starts as the market sprung to life around them, and right in the middle of it all would be my stall, still in darkness, covered by throws. By ten o'clock all stalls should be trading, and those that weren't would face the wrath of Philipus, the market manager. Every morning he stalked through the market, making his presence known, like a cockerel in a farmyard, and if he found any stall shut he would whisk down the sheets, leaving any wares exposed for all and sundry to take what they wanted. Sal and I adored ridiculing Philipus and his attempts at authority, but generally he was a fair man and, more importantly, he was one who could be easily bribed. Chocolate bars and cream cakes could often make up for rent being late. I replied to Sal's text:

'Can you buy Philipus some eclairs? I'll be there in ten. Bus just past Liverpool Street.'

'Ten minutes – you'll be lucky. There's a tube strike today. That bus is going to crawl!' came back her reply.

I looked down at the street, away from the clouds, and saw the road was choked with traffic. Horns were beeping, drivers were fuming, and the couple in front of me had reached new depths of surliness. I made a quick call to Sal.

'Sal, it's me. What shall I do?' I began to laugh.

'What shall I do?' was how I began most of my conversations with Sal as I was usually in some scrape or other.

'Bloody hell, Isla. It's nearly eleven. Time to go home soon!'

'Has Philipus dramatically opened my stall yet?' I asked.

'No, not yet, but he's lingering about somewhere. I can feel him warming up.'

'Do you think the traffic's bad all the way there? What shall I do?' I asked again.

'If I were you, I'd jump off and walk. Actually, no, I'd jump off and run. Sharpish!'

'Alright, I'll see you in a bit.' And I made my way to the lower deck, leaving the couple staring icily out of the window.

I walked through the city's finance district, passing the grand old justice courts, and made my way towards St Paul's Cathedral, where tourists gathered on its steps and pigeons scavenged in the gardens. I left the pungent traffic and walked beside The Thames, stopping at Waterloo Bridge where I waited for the lights to change. Across the river was The National Theatre and Ollie flashed in my mind like the neon lights displaying playwrights and play names across the theatre's concrete face. Ollie had landed his first major role here, playing a young, naive soldier in Arnold Wesker's *Chips With Everything*. I remembered the celebrations we'd had when he landed the part. The pub was packed with his friends and his family cheered down the phone. The red man turned to green and my attention turned back to the market.

It was 10:50. I picked up my phone again and dialled Sal's number. 'Sal, Sal. It's me. Can you do me a favour?'

'Let me guess. Open up your stall?'

'How on earth did you know?' I asked, with fake incredulousness.

'Too late. Will's been already. He's gone and set it up for you.'

Will was the owner of the stall, my boss. He loved life, disliked customers, and had a laid-back charm which attracted most women and threatened most men.

'What did he say? Did he ask where I was?' I asked.

'Doctors, girl! That's where you are. You've got a rash that's spread all over your body. It came on in the night,' Sal laughed, enjoying the subterfuge.

'Shit. I'll be there in five.'

'I'll get you a tea in,' said Sal.

I ran along The Embankment, lined with barges, boats, and pillars from Egypt, and dashed into the Victorian gardens where brass bands played at lunch time and orange carp swam in elegant ponds. Finally I crossed over The Strand and hurtled through a few cobbled side streets that led to Covent Garden. The morning sun lit the piazza like a spotlight on a stage, as both traders and buskers prepared for the day, hoping to line their pockets with gold. Anticipation filled the air like a theatre before curtain call. I flew into the market, weaving through the aisles and sat down at my stall. Sal came over with a tea clasped firmly in her hand.

'Sit down and look busy. Will's back, lurking around somewhere. Peter's just seen him.'

Peter owned the café where we bought our gallons of tea. I sat on my white painted chair and opened up a newspaper, trying to give an impression of calm.

'Your newspaper's upside down.'

It was Will, I recognised his mellow voice, but thankfully there was laughter in it.

I looked at my newspaper and sheepishly laughed.

'How's the rash?' he asked, with knowing amusement.

Before I had time to answer, Sal quickly saved the day interrupting the conversation with trader's talk. 'Have you heard the rent's going up next month?' She shouted across from her stall. Will joined her amongst her teapots, while I dutifully re-organised the stock. Five minutes later he was gone and we were left to drink our tea in peace. The warm air rose beneath the wrought iron roof and Bao, a pretty Chinese girl, gave us both a paper fan from her stall. Talk was of Sal's love life, the web of intrigue she'd woven and was now firmly caught in. Sal had two lovers – occasionally she had three – but at the moment she was down to two: Luigi, a confident yet hapless Frenchman, and Jimmy, a no-nonsense Londoner, who lived in the flat above Sal. The ill-fated French lover had a penchant for dressing in long suede waistcoats, which matched his moleskin trousers. The combination of clothes, along with his jet black hair and pointy, hooked nose, earned him the nick name of 'Goblin'. Sal preferred Goblin when he was far away in France, treating her to wine in Provence and weekends in Marseilles, but when he came to London he was merely a huge embarrassment, who, in Sal's words, '... stank the place out with aftershave, and frightened the life out of the cat.'

But at the moment, Luigi was safely tucked away in France and her life was free from Goblins. It was her ex-husband's gremlins that were causing her problems.

'The ex came round to my flat last night and banged on the door. He'd been on the booze all night,' said Sal. 'Someone had told him about Jimmy.'

'But why would he care? It's none of his business. You've been divorced for years,' I said.

'Jimmy and him were friends. In fact, Jimmy was the best man at our wedding. They fell out badly a few years ago and have never made it up since,' Sal explained.

'So you've known Jimmy for years?'

'I've known him since I was a kid. I wouldn't have minded if I'd been on my own last night, but Jimmy was sat right next to me, larger than life, on the settee. All hell broke loose. Even Mrs Minneapolis came out to see what was happening. You remember her, don't you? Small and Greek with a white deaf cat.'

I did remember the neighbour and her cat. She was a happy old lady, who spoke little English, and lived next door to Sal. She arrived while we were drinking wine one evening, with pots full of stew and smiles and nods in abundance.

'She didn't like all the noise being made and began to shoo the ex away, like a rat.'

The story, like the air around us, grew hotter and even more uncomfortable, and finally ended with Sal's ex-husband declaring his undying love through her letter box, before being shooed away for good.

'What about Jimmy? What did he do?' I asked. Her bizarre relationship with the man upstairs intrigued me.

'Not a lot ... you know what he's like; a man of few words.'

'And does Jimmy know about Goblin?' I was hooked.

'He knows alright – I'm sure. But really it's none of his business. He's never committed to me, and I've never committed to him.'

'Do you want him to?' I asked.

I wondered if she was hiding secret yearnings, but Sal seldom discussed her feelings. The armour she wore against life's setbacks was meticulously polished and very well maintained.

'Maybe, maybe not. He's a funny bloke ... he spent most of his married life with a large plank of wood down the middle of the bed.'

I laughed at Sal's flippant delivery about something so bizarre. She would often divulge small tit-tats of surreal information which would linger in the air between us and stay in my head for days. I still had Jonnie, a young cockney boy who ran the juice bar, dancing around in my membrane, wearing long silky dresses and a blonde curly wig.

'I always thought he was as strange as a child,' she said, and left to tend to her shop.

The afternoon became unbearably hot and we wilted behind our wares like floppy rag dolls. Peter brought tall glasses of iced water from his café to our stalls. We sucked on the ice and splashed the water over our hot faces, laughing like children playing in a fountain. After lunch Will returned with a car full of stock and a weary disposition.

'More tat?' Sal noted, as she filled up her caddies with tea.

Will wasn't in the mood for banter, but Sal's observation was right. Gaudy lampshades, misguided bedroom lighting, and faded paper lanterns tumbled out of the boxes. All of them were items which Will had failed to sell in his shop. He unpacked the goods in silence and grumbled about Sal's blunt London ways.

'I have to hand it to her though. Whatever she's doing she's doing it right,' he conceded, referring to her ever-blooming business. 'How does she do it?' he asked. 'She must have a sixth sense about what people want.'

And it was true, like the uncanny way Sal could read peoples' minds; she had the same intuition about business. But it was many years before she used her talents, as her life had been thwarted by her ex-husband Andy. Andy's philosophy was that a woman's gifts belonged in the home. Over the past few months Sal had given me glimpses into her past, telling me tales which had filled the afternoons with intrigue and had kept the beast of boredom at bay.

She was seventeen when she married Andy and twenty-four when she left him in their small and homely council flat overlooking Leather Lane. Sal was penniless and homeless when they parted, but even though they were married, the law stated that the flat was legally in her husband's name and Sal was merely a signature on a white piece of paper. However, she valued herself enough to live her own life and left him to strut his machismo where and when he pleased.

During the week she worked as a cleaner and at the weekend she helped her father on his stall at The Exhibition Market, selling hammers and nails and other odds and ends. Sal's father was a loud, proud man and had a temperament similar to his daughter's. They laughed as much as they argued, but Sal took to the market life and wracked her brain for something to sell, eventually deciding that what Covent Garden needed was some good old-fashioned English tea. After a year, a small shop came up for sale and she quickly drew up a business plan and flew to the bank. Within weeks Mary's jewellery shop had been transformed into

The Tea Garden, and brightly coloured tea caddies and teapots lined the shelves of Unit 14. Sal never looked back. Her charm and natural warmth, combined with an uncanny intuition, made her the perfect salesperson. Within months Sal's business was one of the most profitable at the market, and as much as this annoyed those who'd been trading for years, it also created a silent admiration. Will was correct: whatever Sal was doing, she was certainly doing it right. But Sal's strongest asset of all was her driving will to succeed. Every tin of tea which made its way into a tourist's bag was another step away from the poverty of her past, adding to her empowerment. Soon she had saved enough money to bribe her ex-husband to leave their council flat and it wasn't long before she was back on her balcony with her plants, her cat, and her pride still intact. Never would she obey another man again.

That afternoon, as Will unpacked the last of his miscreant lampshades, he graciously accepted the market's protocol and indulged in Sal's banter, leaving me to sell his stock to the hordes of tourists who clambered after a bargain; three lampshades for five pounds. They were still arriving at the end of the day, scrabbling through boxes like chickens scratching at corn, when I switched off the lights and covered the stall in cotton Indian throws.

We spent the evening in a stone basement bar, cooling ourselves next to large whirring fans as white wine warmed our spirits. Tonight was Tony's treat, thanks to a win on the horses, and we raised our glasses to Ascot Races and lucky Lady Diva. The summer sky was dark when we left and I zigzagged across the street, hailing a black cab. The warm air hit me as I jumped in the back, and from my bag I took out the paper fan which Bao had given me earlier that day. It was delicate and small and covered in printed rosebuds the colour of raspberries. Before leaving, Tony had given me a crisp twenty pound note to cover the fare.

'I can't have you walking round the East End this time of night,' he had said, 'and to be honest with you Isla, you ain't that steady on your pins right now!'

He was like a kind uncle to me, and I was his eccentric niece whom he would never understand but cared for all the same.

'Good night?' the cab driver asked, as he turned right down Charing Cross Road, past the bustle of Leicester Square.

'It was a great night,' I replied, as the evening air drifted through the window along with laughter and beeping horns.

'Do anything special?'

'I just had a few drinks with some friends after work, down in a basement off Drury Lane.'

'Sounds a laugh to me,' he said.

'It was a laugh. It was a lot of fun.'

It was the first time, in a long while, that I could say these words truthfully. Since I'd been raped I'd only dipped my toe into life, and everything which was going on around me – peoples' lives and day-to-day living – had seemed like a parallel universe. I'd been so lost in my own world of sorrow and mental fatigue that I'd ceased to engage in life. I spent my time half paying attention to conversations, like listening to a radio which wasn't quite tuned in. I picked up words and reality here and there, but they soon became hazy again and I returned back to my own insular thoughts. I perfected the act of saying the right things as needs be, and laughing at the appropriate moments, trying to give the impression of being a 'normal' person; a person who hadn't been raped. I'd been wearing my armour against the sorrow of cruelty, but now I was amongst people who showed so much kindness and camaraderie that my faith in human nature had become stronger than my mistrust of it. Strangers had become friends.

The cab pulled up outside my front door, and its red glossy paint shone beneath the street lamp. I fumbled in my bag for the house keys and let myself in. Suli sprung into the hallway and wrapped herself around my legs and together we stumbled through the bedroom door. She was playful and glad to have company, while I was tired and dying to huddle up beneath my duvet. We came to a compromise and she curled up next to me while I stroked her grey fur and fell asleep, dreaming of wooden planks on floating beds drifting down the Thames.

CHAPTER EIGHT
MARIA

QUITO, ECUADOR, SOUTH AMERICA

18 DECEMBER 1998

Sara and I arrived at the main bus station in Quito, five miles from the centre of the city. It was half an hour past midnight. The sleepy passengers fell out of the bus into the large empty station where two indigenous men had made their beds on wooden benches. Weary and disorientated, we followed the other passengers like sheep, hoping they would lead us to a bus that would take us into the capital. The thought of getting into a taxi still filled us with fear. Was this feeling rational or a manifestation of paranoia? Neither of us knew, but taxi drivers and confined spaces induced an intense wave of panic in us both. It was safer to wait with the other passengers, and so we sidled next to them by a bus stop.

'Quito?' we asked.

A large, elderly woman with a black plait that fell to her waste nodded her head and turned away, staring back into the night. We joined her in her silence and stared out into the darkness. The grey city bus arrived and we sat on its hard, plastic seats, blinking as the lights that lined the motorway passed us by. Shanty towns littered the wasteland, and shelters made from corrugated iron with tarpaulin roofs sprawled across fields as fires blazed in oil drums, like post-apocalyptic settlements. The bus moved onwards towards the outskirts of the capital, passing rubble, tenements, and half-built abandoned buildings before it made its way through the Old Town, down streets lined with colonial houses and Gothic churches. Finally there were signs of life – taverns with people and tables sprawling over the pavements and buskers performing to lively crowds, who jeered and drank, and laughed and smoked. The Old Town was notoriously dangerous, but from the safety of our bus I became mesmerised by the life and activity that hummed through the streets, like a set from a Jacobean play. The stillness of the Andes and its solitary moon were now behind us, and the stimulus of the city careered through me like a drug, diverting my attention away from the intensity of my thoughts. The bus stopped in the new town, at the heart of the finance district, our final destination. Although Quito was clearly a poor city, it had modern amenities: banks, hotels, internet cafés, clubs, restaurants, and bars. There was life. It felt like a capital city, like London. The familiarity brought us some relief, and as we made our way to a hostel down a side street lined with travel agents and tobacconists, I began to feel like I could breathe again. We booked into an old narrow town house, four stories high, and slept in a small room on an old-fashioned bed. Finally we found some sanctuary in our sleep.

The morning brought clear blue skies and a brilliant winter sun, but I had a heavy heart as I drank my coffee in the courtyard, knowing our day entailed a visit to the Embassy and more analysis of the attack. Sara was livelier than I was, talking excitedly about Ali's arrival and the comfort it would bring her, creating an energy that would get her through the morning. But Ollie's arriving wasn't bringing me the same feeling of relief. I knew that Ali had an understanding of intense, overwhelming emotions. The loss and anger he felt when his father died had left him feeling distraught, but he'd worked through his complex feelings with the help of a therapist, and had come to terms with the bereavement. Ollie, however, had little knowledge of such strong, negative emotions, and the thought of his arriving and not connecting with me was making me anxious. Ollie was gregarious, fun, and full of laughter, but I knew listening wasn't his forte. Yet a part of me was questioning whether I was deliberately pushing him away because I was feeling such intense isolation. I'd rather sit alone and be with my own emotions than listen to words of pity or consolation that couldn't change anything, anyhow. Any misunderstanding between us would make me feel worse. I wanted to be solitary – I had been gang raped. I was an outsider now, and Ollie couldn't possibly understand. Not Ollie – a man, an entertainer.

'Let's go,' I said, diverting my thoughts from complications.

We left the sunny courtyard, dropping our keys off at the small reception where a little statue of a smiling Buddha welcomed the guests. Sitting behind the desk was a handsome man with long dreadlocked hair who looked up as we left and smiled, but unlike the Buddha, his smile was weary and his eyes looked distant as we said goodbye and walked out into the street.

The British Embassy was a ten-minute walk away in the heart of the city, next to the heavily guarded Hilton Hotel. The office was of large and open plan, its cleanliness highlighting our scruffy, backpacking clothes, unironed dresses scrunched into rucksacks. A young blond-haired man wearing a white shirt rolled up at the sleeves came to greet us. I recognised his voice. He was the same man I'd spoken to on the phone in Otovalo, and his tone was still gentle. He ushered us into his office and gently explained that the Ambassador of Ecuador had contacted the Head of the Police Department, demanding the immediate return of our passports. At last we had some support, and it came as no surprise that the Ambassador of Ecuador was a woman.

The young blond-haired man spoke again as he pulled out some chairs. 'I don't want to disappoint you, but it's extremely unlikely that these men will ever be caught. I'm sorry. I don't want to get your hopes up.'

I don't have any hope left in me to get up, I thought. I have fury and disillusionment, but not hope, and I hadn't even had thoughts about justice. The only idea that consumed my mind was to reclaim the power the rapists had stripped from me. It was me versus them. I was using all of my willpower not to fall to pieces. I would not let them take away my sanity. I had to stand upright and fight. If I gave up and gave in, their faces would seep from my thoughts into my soul, and sadness and despair would be etched into me, changing the landscape of my life forever. I pictured their vile, ugly faces laughing as they raped.

'I have to at least try and find them. I can't possibly give in.'

'Very well,' he said, 'there is one lawyer in Ecuador who has managed to have a rapist convicted. Two French girls were raped but she found him. It seemed like an impossible task, but she did it. Her name is Maria.'

Again, it came as no surprise that the person passionate enough to track down a rapist was a woman. The gently spoken man rifled through his files for her phone number and made an appointment the same day.

'Two o'clock,' he said and told us that unfortunately we were going to have to give another statement. 'I know it's traumatic for you, but it's necessary.'

And once again we re-lived the experience as the receptionist typed down the details, but unlike the grim, sweat-stained policeman in Otovalo, he offered us sympathy and visibly flinched when I described the rapes.

Before leaving we handed over the evidence: strips of tape, blue, electrical wire, and a plastic clear bottle. They were all placed inside a large plastic bag, sealed and labelled, and locked inside a cupboard in a stark room with white walls and a strip light. I wondered what other evidence was gathering dust in the cupboard and what kinds of objects were waiting their turn for DNA testing. Bloodstained clothes, cigarette butts, knives, and broken glass? Would they always remain sealed and labelled, never reaching the point of forensic testing in a country where life wasn't given a chance to be precious? Murder, it appeared, was not viewed as an atrocity in Ecuador; it was more like something that people prayed would never happen to them. I imagined that the cupboards were probably full of evidence that would stay there until the cases were officially closed. I couldn't imagine the Ecuadorian police rushing to find justice. We signed some forms and wandered back into the cool air and daylight.

Before meeting the lawyer we drank coffee in a street café and tried to eat some food, but our stomachs were knotted and our appetites had shrunk. Sara began to chatter like a small, startled sparrow caught in a storm, but I was too tense to talk and my chest was too tight. Her constant stream of words began to irritate me. I wanted to scream. Both of us were dealing with our stress in different ways. I was internalising mine, Sara was expending hers through words, but together we were creating disharmony.

Maria's office was in the Old Town, on a street that led from the grey medieval Cathedral, layered with centuries of dust and decades of fumes. Blind beggars, like puppets without strings, lay crumpled in street corners and children were left to fend for themselves. An old woman with bones protruding through her skin like tree roots crawling through soil called out as we passed. We placed some money in her lap and rang on Maria's bell, hoping for justice in a country of inequality.

Maria's office was on the third floor of a tall town house which had known more lavish times. Once ornate and grand it was now a relic of riches past. We rang on the brass bell and a slightly built woman in her early thirties answered the door. Her hair was a mass of dark curls, and her dark brown eyes looked at us through circular rimmed glasses.

'Hi, I'm Maria. Come in, come in. There's no lift, just stairs ... Come in, come in.'

She spoke gently but quickly, as though we were running out of time or she was telling us a secret that shouldn't be overheard. She hurtled up the staircase, two steps at a time, and we followed behind, propelled by her energy like a vacuum. The stairs were covered with a threadbare red carpet and the building smelled of a musty antique shop, reminding me of vintage boutiques back home, full of fifties dresses and costume jewellery. Maria opened the door and a man in his sixties with wavy grey hair jumped up from his chair to shake our hands. His presence, like his handshake, was solid and comforting.

'My father, Herr Schmidt,' Maria said. 'He is German, unlike his children who are all Ecuadorian.'

'Sit down, please,' he offered and he pulled out two leather armchairs.

Her father differed in stature to Maria. He was tall and large-boned, but he had the same round face and full lips which gave them both a friendly demeanour. Sara and I both accepted a coffee, but before we had taken a sip, Maria had started her questioning. For the second time that day we told our story, but this time Maria wanted different details, intricate descriptions of the rapists.

'They were dressed casually, smart almost. Long-sleeved shirts, blue thick denim jeans, and they stank of aftershave. One of them had yellow teeth and a front tooth which was gold ...'

'Polizei!' Maria shouted out. She and her father instantly fell into a loud, heated discussion in German.

'We believe it was the police who raped you,' she said, running her hands through her curls. 'The description you gave us shows the men have wealth. Good clothes, cosmetic teeth, aftershave. There are very few people who can afford such luxuries – the military and the police. You told us the police station shut down while you were in town; they were probably scared you might cause them trouble. I have no doubt the rapists were related to the police in Otovalo – the major way into the police force is nepotism.'

Maria played with the pen she held between her fingers, finally putting it down on the desk in front of her. 'If I were you, I'd have them killed.'

'How?' Sara asked immediately.

'I have friends you can pay for a small fee. They will pose as tourists at the top of Mount Mojanda and wait every day until the rapists return, which they will – I know it. But we will be waiting for them, hiding by the road. Just like they were hiding and waiting for you. But this time, we shoot them. It's very simple. Bang – they're dead. The end of three pieces of shit.'

I fumbled in my bag for a cigarette as I toyed with the idea. 'Isn't there another way of catching them?' I asked.

'Yes. You pay me for my time and I'll interview the locals, the Otovalan police, people who've been in prison or have just been released. I'll see if they match your descriptions. I will take the normal approach, but I imagine my investigations won't lead anywhere. People don't like to talk. As I said, it is easier and far more effective if you have them killed.'

A lullaby of voices outside drifted through the open window like a dreamy overture to an intense play. A weird dream was unfolding around me; I felt completely removed from reality. Here in this warm and homely room, festooned with books, paintings, and small Aztec ornaments, I was being asked to take part in a murder. Maria stepped back into the dream.

'Isla, if I were you I'd want them dead. They are fucking worthless! Why keep them alive?' She shouted the words, fierce with rage.

This was not just about my revenge, it was also about hers. She poured out her grievances, anger and despair.

'This country is impossible; it's a police state. There is no diplomacy, equality, or law. They run this fucking country.' She was distressed, tapping the pen on the desk in front of her, trying to dissipate her anger, but her fury was too strong to withhold. 'Every few months I get followed by the police. They trail me to my car from here, this building. They wait until it's quiet and then they pull out a gun, and next they demand everything from me. I don't carry much now ... they took a ring from my mother,' she faltered, and her voice began to break. 'But this is not the point. The facts are they do what they want when they fucking want, and usually to women. They are fucked-up power-crazy pigs. I'm so tired of it. Women are tired of it. Why let them live?'

Her fury had swept through the office like a sandstorm, whipping away the surreal dream, and bringing us back to the present. It was true – why should I let them live, and I honestly couldn't care if they were dead. If their truck disappeared off the side of a mountain, if a freak bolt of lightning burned them all to bones, or a gigantic wave drowned them at sea, I wouldn't give a damn. But to actually pay someone to do any of these things was a different ideal ... to be accountable for another person's death was something I didn't think I could have tormenting my conscience for the rest of my life. Like the third man who stood by me, I didn't want to be part of a vicious and fatal attack.

I liked Maria, and I would have loved to have flown with her passion and to have agreed to her visions of revenge, but I wasn't sure if I believed in a dog-eat-dog mentality. Yet there was a huge part of me that wanted to, and there was a rational part of me that knew there were three dangerous men, somewhere in the Andes, who were free to rape again. To kill the men would halt them in their tracks, but would this compensate for the atrocity of murder? Would their ghosts haunt my dreams? Sara could read my reticence.

'We'll talk about it tonight over dinner,' she said to Maria.

'Do you want them dead?' I asked her.

'Yes, I'd be happy to have them killed,' she replied.

'It's your decision,' Maria said. 'Come by when you've made up your minds.'

We left the charged atmosphere of the office and stepped outside into twilight. The sun's fading rays eased our passions and the breezy air cleared our minds and cooled down the office workers as they caught their buses home. It was Friday, the end of the working week, and an air of jubilation hung in the Old Town, spurring us onwards, past the restaurants, banks, and derelict buildings, back to our hotel.

The dreadlocked receptionist was now behind the small bar. He served us our drinks and asked about our time in the continent. I was evasive and told him we'd been hiking in the mountains. I couldn't bear to repeat the story again, but Sara told him everything. She spoke quickly and incautiously, her words flowing out like a pent-up stream of consciousness as tears fell down her freckled cheeks. As I held her, the barman apologised for his continent, just like the sombre doctor had done in Otovalo.

'I am so sorry you came to this country to explore and unfortunately you found out the truth.'

I didn't say much in response – I couldn't. Rape wasn't

something I could chit chat about over a drink. I would rather not speak at all than speak about something so personal over a beer, in the corner of a bar, on the backpacker's trail. I lit a cigarette, hoping the conversation would move on, and fortunately the phone rang. The dreadlocked man ran through to the reception, past the happy smiling Buddha and picked up the receiver. I took this as a cue to leave and slid off the bar stool before stepping out into the night.

The air was cold, the night was clear, and the stars glowed above the city like miners' lamps searching the sky for seams of gold. We looked for a restaurant and chose a simple Spanish Taverna, with a façade of whitewashed brick.

Inside it was like a cavern, with wooden rustic tables and hand-painted plates hanging from the walls, smooth and bright and large enough to serve a whole family. On the tables were brown pot jugs full of water and two small tumblers made from clay. We chose to sit in the corner, away from the window, and retreated into our own private world, discussing the rapists' fate. The wine warmed our cheeks and quickly allowed our true desires to quell our consciences. It soon became clear we both wanted them found, maimed, and shot dead. We picked at our food and chewed over the consequences of having them murdered.

As far as we could see there were two main problems, the first one being that it could go wrong. Whoever posed as the hapless tourists might be shot by the rapists and killed. We'd have innocent peoples' death on our consciences. The innocence of my world had already been destroyed. Did I need any more darkness?

'They know the risks involved,' Sara said, 'they're getting well paid. It's a job to them. They don't have to do it.'

Sara was right. In South America, life was cheap. Death was a huge part of life, yet life itself could be prolonged and eased with money. One thousand pounds was an amount worth taking a risk for.

'Do you think they're professional hit men or Maria's friends, desperate for cash?' I asked.

'Who cares? Whoever they are, they've decided to take a risk. We're helping them. They'll be able to feed their family for years to come.'

Walk away. Rise above it, and walk away. The telepathic words I had spoken to the third man came back to me, the language I'd tried to send him while kneeling in the thick khaki grass as the wind swayed and bent the blades.

Walk away from this, and rise above it. Don't be a part of this. You will become as low and as vile as they are.

The words had whirled around my consciousness as I lay awaiting the third man's choice.

They want you to do this, don't you see?

'Wouldn't we be lowering ourselves to their level?' I asked Sara.

'I think we would be, in a way,' Sara agreed, 'but I want them to feel how we felt. Just for a moment, I want them to know how it feels to think you're going to die.'

There was silence as the waiter cleared away our plates. I ordered a coffee to focus our minds. 'There's a second problem,' I said. 'If this backfires, we could end up spending the rest of our lives, squandered in an Ecuadorian jail.'

'Why?' said Sara.

'If they trace their deaths back to us.'

'Who'll trace it?'

'The police. If Maria is right, and the rapists are policemen, then soon there'll be three dead ones on top of a mountain. Someone will have to pay.'

'Will they?' questioned Sara. 'Isn't it more than likely that it'll just be a case of another three dead people in a country where murder is rife? Will anybody really care?'

'They could pin it on us regardless,' I said.

'How can they if there isn't any evidence?' Sara's voice was raised now through desperation.

'A judge could very easily be bribed over here. They wouldn't need evidence, just enough money to point the finger at you, me, and Maria,' I explained.

'Maria wouldn't have suggested it if she thought we might end up being caught. She'd be putting her life at risk. It would be utterly ridiculous.'

This is ridiculous, I thought. This whole fucking thing is ridiculous. 'Let's sleep on it,' I said, exasperated. 'I'm too tired to think any more.'

'Okay, let's ask Ollie and Ali tomorrow,' Sara said, and I

nodded in agreement.

'I can't wait to see him,' she added.

'Me too,' I said out loud, but in my mind all I was thinking was please don't let me down.

CHAPTER NINE
BE MY VALENTINE

COVENT GARDEN, LONDON, ENGLAND

14 FEBRUARY 2003

Marcus's mood was as dark as the winter morning, and his words were even icier. It was St Valentine's Day. The tubes were full of commuters clutching roses and the streets were lined with bars and restaurants enticing lovers to swoon over candlelight and crème brulee. The traders had decorated their stalls with flowers and hearts and anything else alluding to love, but customers were scarce in the bleak midwinter, and there wasn't so much an air of love and harmony reverberating around the market, but more of a feeling of grinning and bearing it. Yet it wasn't the lack of money in Marcus's life that was causing him to hide miserably beneath his woollen hat, but a lack of love. Specifically Carlos' love. Every rose Marcus had seen that morning had cut him like a thorn and each restaurant he'd perused had poisoned his very essence. The Spanish boy had made him feel like he was walking on air for over a year now, but his love was unrequited and Marcus was no longer defying gravity but had fallen back down to earth with a bump.

'I told you, didn't I?' Sal said. 'Look at him – a face like thunder. That Spanishy is nothing but a user. Look, you can see it in his eyes.'

But all I could see, and so unfortunately could Marcus, were two beautiful brown gypsy eyes that dared you to dance round open fires and fall in love to the beat of castanets.

Marcus was doomed, and as he opened his stall and smoothed down the lace, his furrowed brow became more creased. Every melancholy thought cast a new wrinkle, and although Marcus was a natural performer, today his dark mood was not for show. Marcus didn't want an audience; he wanted to be left alone. His turmoil was real, but just like secrets, emotions were hard to hide at the market. Traders liked to pass the mornings with idle chit chat: how are you, anything new, are you okay?

'I'm sad – piss off,' wasn't really market etiquette, but Marcus said it anyway, never being a man not to speak from his heart.

The morning dragged without Marcus, and by noon, Midday Mary's were calling. The vodka was practically talking to me through the glass bottle. I wondered if Marcus could hear the serenade too. I poured him a drink and took it over to his stall.

He looked up from a place of deep contemplation and gestured me to leave with a flick of his hand. I sat behind my stall again and sipped my drink, the hot and sour taste signifying the end of the morning. As the Tabasco warmed my lips and the alcohol surged through me, Big Ben chimed midday, right on cue. Five minutes later Marcus appeared, still shrouded in darkness, but his hand was held out for a little cup of light. I poured him a Mary into the small plastic cup. Its healing properties were quick to work. Like the Tin Man, Marcus quickly loosened up, but now he needed to find a new heart. His own had been lost, given away on temporary loan.

'Do you believe in true love, Isla?' The alcohol was working well.

'I do, but as I've told you before, there are consequences. Love can come at a very high price, and sometimes, more often than not, you wish you'd never bid for it in the first place. Believe me, Marcus, I have contemplated love and all its aspects from many different angles,' I said.

'I know. I can see that you've been in love. You like to talk about it openly. Only romantics talk in such a way. So who was the man you fell in love with?'

'His name is Ollie, an actor. Shall I tell you about him?'

'No.'

As I said, Marcus was always honest. I left him to his silent musings and went back to my stall and thought about Ollie and love and all its complexities. I met Ollie for the first time at a rehearsal on a cold midwinter night. I was living on a boat at the time, rented from a warm grey-haired man, Simon, who had fought the establishment in the sixties and now earned his living mending 2 CVs in a shed by the boat. Currently, he was away for six months, and I was looking after his cat. The boat was a huge vessel which had sailed into the seas during the Second World War, saving capsized and drowning men. Her name was now Iona and she was the epitome of bohemia: wood burners, cosy cabins, handwoven rugs, impressionist paintings, and a wheel house that looked out across the river and its fraternity of ducks and swans. The scent of smouldering cedar wood still clung to my clothes on the underground as I made my way to the rehearsal of a short film. The film centred on friendship, drugs, clubs, and hedonism. Although I wasn't a clubber, I was occasionally partial to drug-taking, and at the audition I had chatted to the director with much enthusiasm about magic mushroom highs and watching elves come to life in hedgerows while listening to colours and smelling strange sounds. The mushrooms talk, I told him. In fields and on hillsides they ask to be eaten, shouting pick me, pick me, pick me! The director, a young and earnest man, studied me in a rather bemused way, but hired me none the less.

Seeing this was the case, I wondered what other miscreants he'd taken on board and I arrived at Parson's Green tube station feeling both intrigued and excited. I headed out through the leafy terraced streets and pillar-porched houses. The night was dark and cloudless and smoke swirled from chimney pots out across the London sky as russet autumn leaves fell in the breeze onto the pavements below. I wrapped my coat and scarf tighter around me. I was running late and began to walk faster, but the rehearsal had started by the time I'd stumbled into the large practice room. I bleated my apologies and quickly sat down, gathering my thoughts before looking up at the actor sitting opposite me. In front of me was a man in his early twenties, edgily running his hands through his hair, who looked as flustered as I was. Instantly I fell in love.

Ollie wasn't gorgeous, but he was good looking, and he didn't have a taut, statuesque physique but was tall and slightly plump. His hair was fuzzy, his nerves were frayed, and overall he looked like a bear that had just come out of hibernation. Unlike the Spanish boy, he wasn't a man whose beauty you could lose yourself in, nor did he inspire fanciful thoughts of Romany nights and neighing wild horses, yet when I sat down opposite him, I felt like I'd known him all of my life. There are many ideas about love at first sight, ranging from the mystical and the philosophical, to the functional and the biological. The reason is subjective, depending on the person you are.

The mystics, shamans, and tarot card readers will all tell you there is another realm in the universe other than ours; a different dimension where Guardian Angels whisper and ghosts and spirit guides walk. It is said they steer our lives and move our souls so we can learn cosmic lessons in order to grow. And the biggest mover of all is love. Others say that love at first sight is two souls reuniting after lifetimes apart, maybe to put right some wrongs in the past, or to finally be in each other's arms again. It's a pleasant idea. It gives meaning to life. But a scientist will tell you that love and all its wonder is merely a chemical reaction and it takes only three seconds for a person to decide if they find someone attractive. Once they do, they release pheromones which hopefully create an alluring quality. Thus mating occurs and bouncing babies are born and the human race carries on. Whether Ollie was a thwarted lover from days gone by, a man cruelly taken from me by a douse of the deathly plague, or he simply smelled nice and I fancied him, I don't really know. But whatever the reason, I found myself rifling through the script in our break, dying to see if there was a love scene between us that I might have missed, but much to my disappointment there wasn't. So I set my mind to devising ways to manifest a romantic scene in real life.

The film had five other people in the cast, all of whom had panache for taking drugs, and had mastered the art of contempt for more successful actors. Everyone, that is, apart from Ollie. Ollie couldn't muster the anger required for contempt. In his heart he was a peaceful man. He didn't even raise his voice – he fretted a lot instead, about his lines, about the scenes, about tomorrow's filming and yesterday's stills, and all the auditions which could and would go wrong in the future. Ollie was a worrier. But he knew of a very good coping mechanism to deal with his stress and it could be found on tap at The Five Lions, the small Victorian pub round the corner from where we were filming. It was our first discovery of a shared interest, a love of pubs, especially the old ones, with different rooms and open-lit fires and small intimate snugs, where an old man would sit with his dog, sipping his ale and telling stories about his father and ghosts would whisper through the walls.

Ollie drank happily and frequently, which helped him to maintain a vacant sparkle in his eyes. The rest of the cast had a similar affinity with alcohol, apart from Georgia. Georgia found her motivation in amphetamines instead. An attractive, bold actress, she careered around the set with the energy of a cheetah. When she wasn't acting, she worked as a receptionist in a brothel in Soho. It was well paid and flexible, she told us. Anthony, a handsome Scottish actor, asked about discounts.

Anthony, like Georgia, had a strong inner confidence when it came to acting. Unlike Ollie and me, who both shared a tendency towards neuroses, he didn't question himself. Anthony strode onto the set with the surefootedness of Rockefeller. Oh my God, I can't do this ... What if I'm awful? ... What if I clam up ... oh no, this is a nightmare ... I'm not doing it ... I can't. These were the feelings that me and Ollie knew so well, whereas it would never occur to Anthony that things could go wrong. Worrying was the second thing that Ollie and I found we had in common.

Kim, the fifth actor, was also from Manchester, as Ollie was. He was good looking and boyish, with thick, dark hair and a wry smile that made you wonder where he had been the night before.

Filming took place over a week, in a large comfortable flat, down a leafy Notting Hill street. The owners had vacated their home, renting it out to a film crew for a large sum of money, but after a week of camera tracks running across the luxurious carpets, and actors and crew loitering on armchairs, the middle-class comfortable home had been transformed into an inner-city train station, and had inadvertently been exposed to vandalism. Anthony had accidently pulled a large wooden door off its hinges while using it as a back-stretching device. Anthony was drunk. He had spent his lunchtime at The Five Lions and was now paralytic. Screen acting often involves a lot of hanging around until your scene is ready to be filmed, which can become rather tedious. Some actors spend this time in peaceful surroundings, finding a quiet room to relax in, leafing through magazines, meditating calmly, or practising yoga. But not on this set. Each and every one of us was like an octopus, wrapping our tentacles around as many drinks and drugs as we could find in our ocean of happy hedonism and lust for life. Quiet time out was an alien idea, a mystical concept; something which Buddhists did on top of Tibetan mountains, or a strange notion that would make an interesting article in a Sunday newspaper supplement. Who could blame Anthony for his accidental door-wrecking? The director had hired us for our knowledge of narcotics, hoping our lives would bring authenticity to our characters. Unwittingly he had given us carte blanche to carry on nurturing our expertise on set. Anthony had been methoding away in the corner of The Five Lions and was now pulling doors off hinges, howling with laughter. Fits of giggles ensued on set.

There are few actors who don't giggle on set. The intensity in a scene between two actors can create such a palpable tension that it needs to be dissipated by fits of childish giggling. This is known as 'the nervous giggle'. But there are other types of giggles, brought about by various different situations. Uncontrollable, inane laughter can be brought on when the actor steps outside their character for a short space of time and realises they are staring intensely into another person's eyes, pretending to be someone else. All around the UK there are people beavering away in offices, nurses saving lives, policeman patrolling the streets, and shopkeepers stocking their shelves. Yet somewhere there is an actor, caked in make-up, staring earnestly at somebody else. Suddenly the strangeness of the situation overcomes you and a small smirk begins to form on your lips, and then the other actor begins to crack. This is known as 'the surreal giggle', which usually turns into the infectious giggle that grows into bursts of laughter and ends with a director threatening to give you back your P45 and the crew staring at you in disbelief. There is a job to be done, they are thinking. We are way off schedule, and there's no time for take after take while thespians childishly giggle. But actors are childlike and playful by nature. Why else would they choose the profession in the first place? To spend their lives playing? However, their light-hearted natures don't often make much money and their childlike ways are often curtailed. Soon they find the boards they tread are usually the ones at the Jobcentre, and the only audience they have is a captive one, in the form of a flatmate, who sits and listens resignedly to another tale of telesales woe.

But at the moment we all had a week of paid work, and unfortunately the week was passing too quickly. Time was ticking by, and I had gained little ground in my quest to win Ollie's heart. There wasn't any time left for moonlit walks or subtle hints that would gently fall by him, like petals of apple blossom drifting from trees. This situation needed more than hints. It needed copious amounts of alcohol.

On the penultimate night of filming, Ollie and I were in The Five Lions again. It was the beginning of December and the atmosphere was warm with the Christmas spirit and Friday night celebrations. I began to ply Ollie with drinks, but Ollie had had the same idea and soon we were drunk. Our feelings for each other were the third thing we found that we had in common. And so that night, as the last orders bell rang and Christmas songs chimed through the rooms, we finally kissed and opened the door to endless possibilities – to love and vulnerability, sorrow and broken hearts, or perhaps a fling and a few weeks of laughter. Who could know where this would end? Maybe it wouldn't; maybe it would last a whole lifetime.

CHAPTER TEN
QUESTIONS WITHOUT ANSWERS

QUITO, ECUADOR, SOUTH AMERICA
21 DECEMBER 1998

The bus dropped Sara and me off at the airport amidst wanderlust travellers and taxi drivers vying for their fares. The building was heavily guarded and only those who were flying were allowed in. We stood behind a tall mesh barrier, crowned with barbed-wire-like thorns, and felt the cool wind blow through our hair and out across the runway. I hadn't envisaged my reaction at seeing Ollie again. I hadn't allowed my imagination to stray there. In fact, I hadn't allowed it to stray very far at all. Nearly all of the space in my mind had been consumed by attempts to stay sane, which meant keeping every thought completely in the moment, and never letting them stray back to the peak of Mount Mojanda.

I'd devised a rota, a doctrine that I kept to like a religious zealot: *Get up. Shower. Leave out towel to dry. Eat breakfast. Read book. If mind starts to wander, read the guide book. Go to supermarket and buy lunch (bread, butter, soft cheese, tomatoes). Cut bread evenly and spread butter thinly. Find a café in the guide book, walk to café, and drink a coffee. After lunch read book ...*

I was purposefully concentrating on every task, refusing to succumb to my emotions, removing them from my day-to-day existence. I had to stay in control. Sara, however, seemed to oscillate between nervousness and excitement as we made our journey to the airport, past Quito's makeshift shanty towns, on the small grey bus.

'I'm worried that me and Ali might not bond again,' she said. 'We haven't seen each other for over three weeks. It's the longest we've ever been apart. Three weeks seems like such a long time. Do you think it does?'

There was innocence about her worry. She was like a child almost, and I smiled and tried to reassure her as I cast my mind back to three weeks ago, the last time we'd seen Ali and Ollie. It was the night before we'd flown to Ecuador. We met with some friends in a small pub in Camden, where an Irish trio were playing fiddles, flutes, and pipes, and sang of yearning hearts and the toil of the land. We drank in an early Christmas, jostling at the bar for pints of Guiness. Outside it was freezing. Another country, a different time, the end of innocence.

'Do you think it'll be okay? Do you think we'll bond?' Sara

asked again.

'Of course, I'm sure you will,' I replied. But I didn't want to talk anymore; I needed to be in silence. Opening the pages of my book, I escaped into another world which didn't involve reality.

The passengers from Heathrow had begun to file out of the airport, recognisable by their pale skin and bewildered expressions born from sudden culture shock. Amongst the tide of people were Ollie and Ali, carrying rucksacks and weary expressions. I knew straight away when I looked into Ollie's eyes that he had no idea about the magnitude of the situation. He didn't greet me with the warmth of a lover, but my actions were the same. Neither did I.

'Shall we get on a bus?' I asked, and we began to walk to the glass bus shelter and tentatively held each other's hands. I took charge of the conversation, deliberately leading it towards practical concerns and away from emotional complexities. As the four of us boarded the bus I told Ollie that we had to go back to the Embassy the following morning and collect our passports and I explained to him how we were expected at Maria's tomorrow at three. I pulled out some Ecuadorian coins from the pocket in my purse and told him how much they were worth. The vegetarian food was limited, I informed him, and maybe we should try some fish, and all the while Ollie played along, taking the money in his hands and asking what he could buy with each denomination. But his blue eyes searched for other answers. What's really going on, Isla? What's swirling beneath this rational behaviour? You have never been rational in your life. Why now? However, nothing was going on, but pure avoidance of exactly what Ollie was looking for, some sign of emotion. Sara and Ali sat opposite us, their faces both freckled. Sara's face was glowing from the springtime sun and the relief of seeing Ali again while his was pale from dark London days where the sun left the sky at four o'clock. His boyish charm still remained though, and his smile was tired but kind. The fondness they showed each other was tender, almost like a father and child. Sara at last could rest her head on his shoulder and finally feel supported. She was attentive to Ali's words as he told her about his journey, and any awkwardness that resided between them soon fell away. Neither the mountain nor the rapes were mentioned.

The bus stopped at Quito's main high street and we all clambered off, thankful for the cool breeze that rushed through the air, carrying litter across the roads. The street we were staying at had sprung to life during the morning, and waiters hustled for trade as they set out their tables on the pavement, whisking out paper tablecloths, pinning them down with round glass ashtrays. We arrived at the hostel and walked through its open doors, past the smiling Buddha, and made our way up the small winding staircase that creaked as we transcended floors. Sara's room was on the third floor and mine was above; an attic room with slanting ceilings and a skylight over the oak bed covered by an old patchwork quilt, stitched over time by hands which would never know that a couple would wrap themselves in it so eagerly and make love. Afterwards, we were lulled to sleep by the sounds of the city, car horns beeping and voices calling out in Spanish.

When I woke again, the room seemed mustier and darker and my head felt heavy. A large cloud hung above the skylight. Ollie slept next to me. His body was warm and his face had the calm expression of an innocent child. In the hushed room and with Ollie close by, I started to relax and my thoughts began to finally wander, but they wandered back to Mount Mojanda and the rapists, and I began to wonder what had driven them to rape. Sexual frustration? Lust for power? A hatred of women? Or maybe they did it simply because they could. Perhaps the opportunity arose and they acted on it. Maybe it was a natural instinct, a primal urge that evolution hadn't eradicated over time? Once my thoughts had picked up on this theme, they wouldn't stop, and I began to wonder if all men, beneath layers of social protocol, could be rapists. Mankind created civilization, and along with towns and cities came morality, intelligence, and powers of deep thought. But on the peak of Mount Mojanda, where the wind swirled and thick grass grew as high as a horse, had the rapists instincts been stirred, knowing there was no one around to judge them, realising they were free from the constraints of society and far removed from the possibility of ever being caught and vilified? Had they simply given in to their primal urges? Had they meant to only steal from us but their instinct took over? Would every man, given the chance, do the same? If this were true, the third man would not have merely stood by; he would have joined in too. I rubbed my eyes, which were still heavy with sleep, and looked over at Ollie and began to wonder what Ollie would have done. Hypothetically speaking, would Ollie have walked away? I needed to know. I wanted to know who he really was. What lay beneath the charm and the mask of the actor? I turned to him again, but his face showed only serenity. Like the hushed room, filled now with shards of sunlight warming the wooden floorboards, Ollie's face conveyed peace. I got up to find some bottled water and poured myself a glass before climbing back into bed and opening my book where the bus-ticket bookmark was lodged between pages. I tried to read but my eyes wandered over the same paragraph again and again, without absorbing the words. I had to know what Ollie would have done – who would he have stood by, the rapists or the third man? I woke him up and asked him.

'Ollie, is there any part of you that can understand why those men raped me up on the mountain?'

Ollie looked alarmed. 'Are you asking me if I empathise with these men?' he asked.

'No. I'm asking you if there's any part of you that would have done the same thing. Honestly, is there a voice in the back of your mind that says you might have? If there'd been no one around, no comebacks and no chance of prison, and a girl was lying in front of you helpless – would you have joined in? Would you have raped her?'

'Why are you asking me this?' he said.

'Why aren't you answering me?' I replied.

'We're together in bed. It's cosy and we're warm. Why are you asking me this now?'

'Why aren't you answering me? Your answer should be "no". Immediately. "No, I would not partake in gang rape."'

There was a silence in the room, as though a funeral procession had just walked through.

'Please, say no,' I said plaintively. I couldn't tell if he looked bewildered or guilty.

'There's no need to ask me this. You're safe now. Why are you talking like this?' he asked.

'Say fucking no!' I shouted the words at him. 'You're not answering me because you know, deep down, you would have joined in.'

By not answering the question, Ollie was declaring his guilt.

'Isla, stop being so crazy. Please, sit down. Let's talk about this calmly, okay?'

Perhaps Ollie was right, maybe I was descending into madness, but I refused to be placated or patronised and didn't sit down next to him. Instead I walked into the bathroom and splashed cold water over my face, letting it drip carelessly down my neck, cooling my skin and calming my emotions. Why would Ollie consent to rape? After all, it was only one step away from murder ... And I asked myself the same question: if nobody was watching and no one could see me, if there was no one to judge me and there would be no repercussions, would I murder my enemy? Here in this lawless country, where morality was second place to survival, I was being given this chance. The man with the golden tooth and his ugly, vile friend doused in cheap, strong aftershave could cease to exist if I said so. I sat down next to Ollie and asked him what he thought about their possible, imminent murder.

'You can't possibly carry on with your life, Isla, knowing you were responsible for murdering people. It will haunt you for the rest of your life,' he warned me, 'you'd have their dying breaths forever on your conscience.'

'But once they are dead, it's over. Too late for regrets – there'd be no going back and I'd have to accept it. Live with it. Maybe even one day their deaths would be ordinary. There might come a time when I'd forget about them …'

'I don't think you would. I think it would stay with you forever.' His voice was calm.

'But they've filled me with darkness, Ollie. They've abused me. They nearly tried to fucking kill me, so why shouldn't I have them murdered?' The room filled with sadness, silence and contempt. 'Why don't you hate them?' I asked him.

'I just think you'll regret it, that's all.' Ollie's tone was gentle but firm.

He stood up from the bed and crossed the room to unpack his rucksack.

'If this had happened to you, if three men had made you feel so scared and all you wanted to do was curl up into a ball and cry it all away like some fucking awful nightmare, then I'd want them dead.'

'I'm different to you,' he said, while he folded his t-shirts and placed them in the heavy wooden drawers. 'I don't have your fiery nature.'

'Fiery nature, is that what you call it? I'd say it's more like justified anger. I've been gang-raped. Do I have to spell it out to you? Gang rape equals fucking anger.' I shouted the words at him.

'We're different – that's all I meant. We handle things differently,' he explained.

'Why aren't you angry? Can't you feel a real emotion or do you always need a script?' I spat out the words. Ollie looked confused and upset. I was angry and felt instantly guilty. 'I'm sorry,' I said.

Sara knocked on the door. 'Are you ready?' she asked in a carefree voice.

We left the hotel, but our mood came with us and we walked down the side street in silence, passing by cafés now filled with travellers longing for home, or those still filled with wonder, loving the bohemian lifestyle. The tables were now covered with beer bottles and ashtrays brimming with strong unfiltered cigarettes. Ollie put his arm around my waist and gradually the atmosphere between us lifted. The four of us made our way to the major thoroughfare of restaurants, tavernas offering beans and fish, themed wild-west restaurants serving beef and beer, and bistros lit by candlelight that were small, secluded, and fine. Sara checked the menus of each one meticulously.

'There isn't any fresh produce on this one. I think all the food will be frozen ... There are only two things here that sound even edible ... The set menu looks okay, but I wonder if the portions are small?'

She seemed to have lost her perspective; the bigger picture was eluding her. Why would I care whether the fish had been stuffed in the freezer? A week ago I had two guns pressed against my head – the joy of a succulent fresh fish wasn't the major thing on my mind. But Sara was now on holiday, like we were always supposed to have been, and she deserved her right to enjoy herself. Yet for me the trivialities of day-to-day life seemed of little importance any more. Gang rape was a crime – freezing fish was not.

We found a restaurant and sat around a table drinking wine from a glass carafe but very soon the conversation became unbearable. The fish was too salty, the sauce was too thick, the coffee was strong, and the main course was late. The freshness of the salad was analysed by all and the bill was discerned with the beedy eyes of an accountant. I sat in silence, feeling like an outsider. Neither Sara nor Ali had asked me how I was feeling. Was I being excluded because of their unease at confronting the situation, or maybe, as Sara had stated to me a few days previously, we both went through the same thing. If she was fine, then why wouldn't I be? If she could sit and have a viewpoint on the hollandaise sauce, then surely so could I? But I couldn't, and neither could I pretend to. Sara, Ali, and Ollie were ignoring incredible violence and giving me little comfort. I knew for certain that from now on I was on my own.

The following day we returned to Maria's office. The previous night it had been decided we would pursue the case conventionally and the rapists' lives would be saved. The morning had brought another day of clear blue skies and we sat in the shaded courtyard discussing our travelling plans for the next two weeks, the length of time Ollie and Ali were in the country for. I'd considered flying home, but I didn't know what to do when I got there. Here, in South America, my life was on hold. I was living day by day. Like all the other travellers who passed through the reception and ate breakfast in the courtyard, I could drift. It was decided we would head towards the virgin jungle and leave the capital behind. Afterwards Ollie and I would go on to the Galapagos and Ali and Sara would go on their own adventure.

Full from breakfast, we sauntered towards Maria's office. The Old Town was empty. The buskers and beggars had not yet arrived and the rest of the town were working. An old couple passed through the cathedral's wooden doors and the sweet smell of incense escaped into the empty streets. We pressed the bell of Maria's office. She answered quickly, greeting us enthusiastically, before leading us upstairs where she shook our hands and asked us to be seated. Maria's energy surged through her as she darted round the office, picking up paper and pens and boiling the small, plastic kettle.

'Okay, okay. Tell me, what have you decided?' she asked, as she perched on the edge of her antique desk. Her brown eyes darted back and forth between me and Sara.

'We don't think you should go back up the mountain and wait

for the men. We're scared of the consequences,' I said.

And there in Maria's office, with its stacks of books and Aztec artefacts, I spoke the words of a well-brought-up English girl of impeccable virtue, and threw away my chance of sweet and justified revenge. Maria found it hard to restrain her anger.

'The chances of catching them any other way is zero,' she said, her fingers winding themselves through her curls with frustration. 'I will be taking money from you for no other reason than going through the motions of an investigation that will amount to nothing. I ask you to think again.'

My inner voice, my wild side, and the ongoing fatigue I was feeling, urged me to tell her to do whatever she liked, but we had made our decision, and all I wanted to do now was to sail to the Galapagos Islands, as Ollie and I had always planned to.

'Please, Maria. Our minds are made up.'

'Okay ... my first step is to go to Otovalo, interview the locals, and question the police. If I hear anything important I'll contact you by email,' she informed us. We solemnly shook hands and said goodbye.

The four of us walked through the Old Town like ghosts, quietly lost in our thoughts, and found a café where we sat and read the guide book, looking for a place to stay near the virgin jungle.

And so we travelled south to Baños, into the cusp of the rainforest, and stayed in thatched wooden huts and dined with their owner in his humbly constructed home and filled ourselves with pollo sin pollo, white wine, and his peaceful outlook on life. He rarely saw cities but was seldom without company. In the morning we showered naked in a high trickling waterfall and the afternoons were spent trekking through the virgin jungle, looking for animals and searching for birds. Ollie was excitable and laughed as we crossed rickety wooden bridges tied over cavernous ravines, holding hands and not looking down.

I didn't feel back to normal here or in any way sane, but the jungle felt pure, with its lush vegetation and different shades of green. Deep emerald leaves like huge water lilies grew dense and tall through the undergrowth and moss dripped from the branches of trees like olive oil. Everything was untainted and came from the earth, a natural oasis, away from urban progress. In the grassy enclave, where our huts were nestled, some kind of peace descended upon us. A tropical bird with green and yellow shimmering wings perched itself on top of a hut and began to preen its feathers while we lazed on the ground beneath, aimlessly chatting and watching the wandering clouds. A feeling of warmth resided between us, like nomads on the prairie. Sara rested her head on Ali as they talked about her travel plans. They had decided to stay on the mainland.

'Firstly,' she said, 'we're going back to Otovalo to buy some clothes and gifts from the market. Ali wants to buy some jumpers to take home with him as presents.'

I couldn't believe what Sara had just told me; she wanted to go back to Otovalo, of her own free will. Under no duress, she was willing to travel back to a town where two rapists, and in my mind possible murderers, were still roaming free. Otovalo wasn't a metropolis; it was a small market town. There was a strong chance she might see them again. The thought of looking into their eyes for another time filled me with terror.

'I wouldn't set foot in that town,' I told her adamantly, 'not for all the money in the world.'

'It'll be fine,' she retorted. 'We won't be there long, only a night or two.'

I must be going mad, I thought. Is there only me who finds her actions insane? My mind became clogged with doubt. I am going mad – of course I am. Rape is barely a crime and I'm being a drama queen. It's normal. It's natural. It's all part of life, like a horrible accident where you end up in hospital on the operating table. These things happen. But it isn't normal, because if it was the third man would have joined in. The third man knew it was wrong. It is wrong; it's as bad as torture. I didn't want it to happen; it was forced upon me. It's a fucking crime.

Anger surged through me like a streak of freak lightning, but I looked around at my companions' sunny dispositions and stopped my tongue from striking. I moved away from my inner storm and concentrated on the yellow bird cleaning its feathers on the roof of the hut, watching its movements, its tiny beak meticulously gnawing at its plumage. My mind calmed and I tried to work out her reasoning. Whichever way I looked at it, her actions seemed not only dangerous but incredibly disloyal and showed no respect for my feelings. A week ago I was forced to beg for my life on my knees, and now Sara wanted to return to the same town to go shopping, as though her last visit had been unfortunately cut short due to the untimely misadventure of gang rape. I was absolutely incredulous and rendered speechless. The only conclusion I could come to was that Sara was in total denial and was blocking out the event from her mind. Rape, guns, and mountain roads were now far behind her. She had latched on to a happier place: Ali and their future together with babies and a garden full of herbs. Had she created a mental retreat in her mind where the violence she had witnessed was fully blocked out? My thoughts were too scrambled and dark to go to happy places. All I had left was my motivation not to crumble and my refusal to let the rapists win, but meanwhile my friendship with Sara was doing exactly this. It was crumbling rapidly. Like a hand-knitted jumper our relationship was starting to fall apart. Too many pulls at the loose ends, and the whole thing would unravel completely.

CHAPTER ELEVEN
THE INNOCENT ISLES

GALAPAGOS ISLANDS, ECUADOR, S. AMERICA

27 DECEMBER 1998

We flew to the Galapagos Islands in a small plane with a handful of American tourists, a scientist, and a businessman. The scientist was in his mid-twenties and sat on the seat next to me. He'd been on Isabela Island for a year, he told me, studying the cormorants. At first he'd been lonely, but the beauty of the island and the ever-expanding sky had entranced him, and were now a part of his soul. They were now as necessary to his life as breathing. On his wrist he wore a frayed friendship band. The plane landed on San Cristobel, one of the few islands inhabited by man, and the sun shone brilliantly. We made our way to the main town built on the shore and sat on the small beach in between two piers, leaning on our rucksacks, pulling off our shoes, and burying our feet in the warm, fine sand. Huge wobbling sea lions were everywhere, lazing on the decks of fishing boats and the bonnets of cars. They were tame and playful and knew no fear of man, because man had never hurt them and their trust of humans remained intact. We stayed in a small hotel with whitewashed walls and a little stone balcony overlooking the harbour and watched the boats bob and the sea lions roam as the light turned from light blue to violet. That night Ollie cried out and woke from his sleep; his dreams had turned into nightmares.

The next day we boarded Skipper, a small sailing boat, and began our cruise around the islands. On some of the isles we stayed overnight. Others were explored for only a day, their black volcanic rock and barren landscapes jutting from the water as though shards of the moon had fallen into the sea. Marine iguanas sat in peaceful silence, watching the ocean, occasionally knocked from their solitude by the frothy crash of a breaking wave while shoals of dolphins swam by our boat as we sailed between islands, dancing and breaching, their grey shiny skin reflecting the sun like sea jewels. We ventured onto The Isla de la Plata, home of the Blue-footed Booby, a large sea bird with bright blue webbed feet that nested wherever it chose; in the middle of sandy pathways, or on top of rocks and grassy ledges. They too were free from predators, knowing the seals never strayed from the shore. We swam with the seals some days. The younger ones circled round us, enticing us to play, twisting and turning, nudging us gently with their whiskered noses. During the evening we ate supper cooked by our guide on the deck, while an American woman described the beauty of the shopping centres back home.

On the second largest island, Santa Cruz, lived a subspecies of the giant tortoise. A small bus arrived at its harbour to pick up Skipper's passengers, along with other tourists from different boats, wearing shorts and sunhats and eager expressions. The bus jostled its way over rocky roads to a hillside where dozens of tortoises had gathered. The large hill was half covered by a thick morning mist, dampening the vegetation, making it the ideal habitat for the large, shelled creatures. As we clambered off the bus the vapour began to rise, revealing nearly a hundred giant tortoises grazing like dinosaurs would have, millennia ago. We walked up the steep hill to the slow old creatures, but as we approached them they hissed, drawing their wrinkly necks and leathery heads into their shells. Our tour guide told us they were scared of man because man had abused them over the centuries. They'd rammed them into ships and turned them on their backs, killing the creatures one by one, eating their flesh, using their bodies. Here on Darwin's isles it seemed that evolution had had no affect on man whatsoever. Man was still cruel when it wanted to be.

CHAPTER TWELVE
HOME?

QUITO, ECUADOR, SOUTH AMERICA
8 JANUARY 1998

Ollie and Ali flew back to London, and every day became more unbearable. My mind was on constant alert like a soldier at war. There wasn't any peace to be found as stress, anxiety, and bouts of insomnia began to take their toll. With Ollie gone I felt unprotected and vulnerability seeped through me, weakening my resolve to battle. On the streets I walked quickly, averting my eyes from passers-by, convinced that anyone at any moment might grab me and mug me and shoot me dead. But we carried on regardless ...

One hot, dry afternoon Sara and I took a picnic and some books to the Parc Nacional in the centre of the city where office workers ate lunch and teenagers strummed guitars and puffed on weed. We found a spot beneath the drooping branches of a budding tree and lay down a blanket. A man sauntered towards us as we unpacked the olives, bread, and cheese.

'Hi! You guys been in Quito long?' he asked. He was an American, in his early thirties, and spoke in a laid-back manner.

'We just got back a few days ago. Isla was in the Galapagos and I've been up to the Andes,' Sara said.

'Wow. I'd love to go to the Galapagos, but I don't think my budget's gonna stretch that far,' he said, adjusting the strap on his shoulder bag as he spoke.

I didn't like him being so near to us. I felt like our space was being invaded and I began to panic. My stomach contracted, as though a snake was coiling around it, stopping me from breathing. The American adjusted the strap again and I could feel my chest tighten. Why does he keep fiddling with his bag, I thought? What's he so nervous about? What's he hiding? What the fuck is he carrying? He's got a gun. Fuck, he's got a gun in his bag.

'Run. He's going to kill us!' I cried and pulled Sara up off the rug and ran as fast as I could all the way back to the steely gates of the entrance. I leaned against the railings crying, trying to catch my breath.

'He was a fucking weirdo, Sara. He was going to shoot us.'

Sara looked at me with her large violet eyes full of concern. 'I don't think he was,' she said. 'I think he was just being friendly.'

After lying down for an hour at the hostel, staring at the ceiling from my bed, I came to the conclusion she was right. Despite our fragile mental states we carried on making plans to travel further into South America. If I carried on travelling I could delay my inevitable return to London, knowing that when I got home it would feel like the end of an era. I could no longer act or work and sail on life's unpredictable waves of joy and sorrow with the passion and enthusiasm that I used to. Like an empty crystal ball, the future held nothing. Travelling was a transient place of limbo.

We decided to go to Paraguay, where Sara's father had lived as a child, and then on to Chile where snow fell on plains where man seldom trod. Before we'd set out to this continent, I'd set my heart on seeing wild spectacle bears swinging in trees and had imagined spending nights in the wilderness on arctic adventures, sleeping in small igloos, with a guide and fellow travellers, building fires outside in the night. I wanted to maintain the dream and feel that life still had some meaning.

A few days after the picnic, another incident happened that gave us insight into our mental instability. Sara and I were taking a taxi home from a restaurant above a shop selling leather saddles and horse riding boots. Up until now we had not dared to be alone with a man in a taxi, but the dimly lit side streets where only the occasional street lamp threw any light were making us anxious. As we got into the taxi, the middle-aged driver spoke to us in Spanish. His tone sounded abrupt, but we hadn't understood his words. He pulled out into the traffic, shouting at the driver of the car in front, repeatedly stabbing his horn. Again, he spoke in his native language, louder this time, his dark brown eyes staring at us both through his rear view mirror. We replied in phrasebook Spanish, saying we were sorry, but we didn't understand. He banged his fist on the side of his window and spat out some words. His voice was loud, raised in anger.

'I want to get out! Let me out,' Sara shouted. 'LET ME OUT.'

She tried her door but it was locked. I pulled the handle on mine, but the door didn't open.

'Stop! Stop now. Stop the car,' I shouted.

'Give him some money. We need to give him some money,' Sara said.

She grabbed her bag and pulled out her wallet, throwing a large handful of notes at him. Whatever the amount was, it was enough to make him veer over to the side of the road. The car stopped and he unlocked the doors. We escaped and ran down the street to our hostel where Sara burst into tears.

'I'm going home tomorrow,' she said. 'I'm going to the airport and I'm going home. I can't take it anymore.'

That night we drank cheap brandy in the hostel bar. The alcohol gave us fortitude and calmed our nerves, and as Sara relaxed she began to find a happier state of mind, talking about her future with Ali again, describing their plans to move to Bristol and one day start a family. I was utterly indifferent to where I lived, as wherever I was, my thoughts of violence would always come with me. As I tried to sleep that night, I wrapped myself in soft blankets and wished I was back in Parson's Green on a cold November night dowsed with the scent of autumn leaves, where I'd walked into a rehearsal room and fallen in love with a young, blue-eyed man whom I felt like I'd known all my life. I wanted excitement again, fearlessness and wonder, but instead my emotions felt as dead as the dying. That night I dreamed of bears disappearing into drifts of snow.

The following morning we packed our rucksacks and caught the bus to the airport. We sat in silence, hung-over from the brandy, and watched the city, seeped in poverty, history, and a lifetime of memories, passing us by for the very last time. The airport was busy, cool, and clean. We spoke to the steward at the Information. His English was perfect and his efficiency graceful. Within minutes we were booked onto the next flight to Heathrow. Finally, we were going home.

It was daylight when our plane took off and dusk when it landed in Aruba, a Caribbean island drenched in balmy heat and the scent of tropical flowers. The Arubians spoke in soft, slow voices which matched their mellow mannerisms. No longer were we surrounded by staccato accents – strong, clipped, and fast. Ecuador and its urgency were now far behind. As we waited for the plane to refuel, we watched the other aircrafts take off and land through the large departure-lounge windows. Our last portal to transience. An hour later we were back on our plane, flying through brightly lit stars and passengers' dreams. We watched American sitcoms on a screen in the middle of our aisle, and landed in the early hours of the morning, with the sky still dark with winter. Rubbing our eyes and pushing our rucksacks on steel trolleys through strip lights and customs, we ventured out into the hub of Heathrow and down into the warren of the Underground. A wave of anti-climax ran through me. There wasn't a guide book to follow anymore and there were no more adventures we could pretend to have. I was no longer passing through; I'd reached my final destination. But home didn't mean anything to me anymore and all its connotations slid away as quickly as the tube doors opened.

I sat on the tube, along with night shift workers from the airport, and read the English adverts above the seats. On the top of Mount Mojanda I never imagined I'd see London again, or sit on the underground with its prickly checked seats. On top of the peak, with our wrists bound together and our mouths full of tape, I never even thought I'd see the farmland at the bottom of the mountain. And now, here I was, sitting next to Sara with her head resting on her rucksack and all I wanted to do was hold her and thank her and tell her that without her I would never have got home that night. Without her patiently leading me down the endless rubble road and clasping her small hand over mine, I wouldn't have had the courage to move. But as we travelled together, our journey as friends was drawing to a close and Sara left me at the Northern line, with a hug and a 'Will you be okay?'

'See you later,' she said, 'I'll call you.' And she disappeared up the escalator.

It was still early when I arrived at Finsbury Park station. I walked through the long concrete underpass and showed my ticket to the inspector in the booth. He waved me through the gate and out into the freezing February morning where snow had turned into murky black ice. The sky was grey and the bus station quiet. The commuters were now all at work and nobody else had ventured out into the cold winter day. I found the bus stop to Golders Green and sat on the narrow metal bench beneath the Perspex shelter, opposite a road of kebab shops, bookies, off-licences, and newsagents. An empty fast-food box drifted past me with a smiling chicken on the front and cellophane cigarette wrappers littered the street. My heart sank and I longed to be back in Ecuador, amongst the colourful markets and its clear blue skies and the promise of every day bringing something different. Away from the transient life of travelling, I had to face my future, and whichever way I looked at it, the reality was that my future looked bleak. Like a soldier back on civvy street, I had no idea how to start my life over again, and longed to go back overseas. I reached inside my rucksack and pulled out a thick llama-wool scarf. Wrapping it around me, I had never felt so alone in the whole of my life.

For the first few weeks I stayed with Ollie in his small flat above a shop in Golders Green. At the time I was living with my close friend Kate, but Kate worked away and our flat was empty. The thought of being alone was more than I could bear but Ollie had accepted a leading role at The Hampstead Theatre and spent most of his days rehearsing, and so I spent mine with my close friend Barney, seeking company and avoiding the void of fear.

I'd known Barney ten years, since Sixth Form College days, where we'd met and formed a band together, which finally took us to London. Barney, with his floppy brown hair and wanderlust stare, was my closest friend. I knew him implicitly. His kindness was immeasurable, and his easy-going nature almost ethereal. After returning from Ecuador I spent my days talking with him, drinking cups of tea which we replaced with bottles of beer as soon as the night came. His flatmate, John, was our mutual friend and between them they spent their time distracting my mind, making me laugh, and we all played 'Mario Cart' on Barney's N64. I slept a lot of nights in his flat, and in the morning I talked about the rapes to the Metropolitan Police as I gave my statement for a third time in a modern police station near Kilburn Park. Barney and John's company helped me through the day and their humour got me through the night. We all became partial to the off-licence around the corner that served until the early hours. Sometimes I was sick and sometimes I wasn't.

After three days of intensive interviews I signed the statement and the police handed the case to Interpol who allegedly investigate crimes abroad. Until I heard from Interpol, I was relying on Maria to bring me good news, and until I heard from Maria, all I could do was passively wait.

The days I did see Ollie were long and fraught with friction. The opening of the play was approaching and his lines were still evading him. His memory was failing and his anxiety grew. He visited the doctor, who prescribed him drugs to slow his heart. He saw an acupuncturist, who unblocked his chi with needles, but his nerves wouldn't rest and he couldn't relax, and every evening Ollie paced the living room floor, overlooking the lamp-lit street like a bear in a concrete cage. Whereas once I would have supported him, I had no more sympathy to give. To my ears his complaining sounded like a rich woman in an orphanage bemoaning the fact she'd broken a nail. He was too anxious to see a bigger picture, and I was too low to care about his play. The more he complained, the angrier I became, and his lack of concern for me lowered my opinion of him. Resentment filled the days and I spent the nights drinking, telling friends one by one about the rapes and my fractious friendship with Sara.

The friend I confided in first was my oldest friend, Kate, with whom I was meant to be sharing a flat. Ollie and I met her in The Bush, a large, old pub in Hampstead with framed theatre posters from the fifties and tall-standing lamps with tassels like necklaces. Kate had been wondering why I'd come back from South America so early, and she was also curious to know why I hadn't stayed a night at the flat.

'I know I like things tidy,' she joked, 'but you can actually live there. I won't hoover you up.'

Kate was my oldest friend; we'd met as eleven-year-olds at secondary school. Kate was rebellious and I was mischievous and together we'd found a shared love of freedom that had fused us together as friends. Neither of us had much respect for authority and our high spirits had got us through our school days, which we'd both looked upon as a prison sentence. Kate was robust, direct, and liked to hear things straight.

'Kate, I've got something to tell you. It's going to really shock you,' I said.

'You're pregnant?' she guessed.

'I was gang-raped in Ecuador.'

Kate searched my eyes. 'This isn't true,' she said, 'it can't be.'

'I'm afraid it is.'

Kate was as silent as drifting snow. 'This is awful,' she said. 'This is fucking awful ...'

She put her arms around me. 'I'm so sorry,' she said.

'So am I,' and we both began to cry.

'It's the first time I've heard you go quiet,' I said, and laughed.

Kate laughed too. And then we cried. And then we laughed some more and then we sobbed.

Ollie's play opened to mixed reviews, but he managed to keep his nerves at bay and the press praised his performance. I waited until the third night before going to see it, giving him a chance to warm into his part. Afterwards he introduced me to the cast. Whereas once I used to love actors and their exuberance, I now felt uneasy amongst them. There had been a time when I'd belonged with them, but now I felt like an outsider looking in on a world which felt strange and distant, like an adults' world might appear to a child. I was aware they might have been thinking I was morose or downhearted, dour or incredibly serious. Ollie's introverted girlfriend. I wanted to speak to them and blurt out my thoughts. I'm not usually like this, but I'm suffering from shock. I've just been gang-raped – do you see...? But gang rape caused awkwardness and once more I felt gagged.

'What do you do?' asked the fifty-year-old lead.

'I was an actor too, but I can't see me doing it again for a long time ... I've lost a lot of confidence,' I replied.

As he spoke to me in a deep and mellow tone, the kindly actor put his arms around me. 'I know exactly what you mean – stage fright was it? It happened to me. Don't worry, you'll get through it. I've got a brilliant self-help CD. Visualisation and all that, a bit Californian, but it worked. You can borrow it if you like? I'll give it to Ollie. It helps combat the fear.'

'Thanks,' I said, and he wandered off looking for a more enthusiastic audience.

The theatre shut its doors for the night and the party of actors and the young, dark-haired writer moved from its foyer into the pub across the road. The actors carried on with their lively conversations, gesticulating with their arms and hands, performing to the other drinkers sitting at tables, or idly reclining in old battered armchairs. I sat next to the quiet writer, knowing he would be happy to talk with me about his play, hoping we would be left alone. But before long a member of the cast with a voice as smooth as liquid chocolate came to join us and asked me who I was and what did I do. I made my excuses and left him talking about act two and bought a glass of white wine at the bar, just before the clock chimed eleven, heralding last orders. We downed our last drops of alcohol and smoked our final cigarettes before setting out into the cold winter night. Ollie was on a high and he smiled with delight at having got through another performance, and when Ollie smiled, his gentle and happy nature radiated from him. Even the winter outside lost its severity.

We hailed a black cab from the ring road that led to the North. I sat in the back, watching the cars go by and the double-decker buses filling with passengers wrapped in big coats. I wondered where they'd come from and where they were going to. Had their nights been fun or formal? High art or hedonistic? I lost myself in their worlds and thought about the road that led to the north of England and how much I wanted to go home to York.

The taxi stopped at some traffic lights and a motorbike pulled up next to my window. The rider was a broad-shouldered man, dressed in a leather jacket and riding boots the size of two small ships. His black visor covered his face and he revved his engine, eager to move on with his journey. Suddenly he looked at me and I turned my face away. I looked again, but his visor was still facing in my direction, large, faceless and menacing. I panicked and couldn't breathe. He's going to kill me, I thought. He's going to pull out a gun and shoot me through the window in the face. I felt sick. Fuck off. Leave me alone. I took a deep intake of breath. Fuck off. The traffic lights turned amber and he sped off to his destination. I turned to Ollie, who was staring out of his window, lost in a daydream, unaware of my private nightmare. We both now inhabited different worlds, repelling like magnets, opening the door to living like strangers.

I spent the next day with Barney, helping him with his rounds as a part-time removal man, lugging around furniture. The work supplemented his income as a musician and kept me and my dark mind occupied. I felt safe in Bertha, the bottle-green transit van, eating cheese and onion pasties and drinking coffee out of plastic cups, bought from garages en route to people's homes. I helped him out the following day, and the next day after that, and on the third day, for a change of scenery, I took a shortcut to his house down an ordinary inner city suburban street; a mixture of sixties' council blocks and modern houses lined with trees and a couple of shops. Stationary cars sat by the curb and a dog barked in the distance. The noise sounded like the creature was locked in a yard, its yelp echoing around the confined space. The grey winter sky weighed down oppressively and the street began to take on a sinister air. It was lifeless and quiet and lacked any joy. My mind went back to darkness. A man's going to come calmly out of his door and pull me off the street. He'll drag me into his house, inside his hovel, into a cell full of torture implements, and no one will ever hear me scream, and I'll die of starvation, tied up in a dark room without any daylight. Day in, day out, year after year I'll be in his disgusting, filthy lair. STOP THESE IRRATIONAL THOUGHTS. But they're not irrational, are they? People are cruel. People are evil. I know this; I've seen it. I've witnessed their depravity. I've stared the fuckers straight in the eyes. It's never going to happen again. I won't let anyone get me ever again.

I dialled Barney's number.

'Hi lovely. Are you okay?' he asked.

'No, I'm not. I'm freaking out. Please come and get me.'

'Where are you?'

'The street, near the park, next to your road.'

'What's going on?' Barney asked, trying to remain calm.

'It's quiet, there's no one around. I'm scared.'

'Carry on walking,' he said, 'and I'll stay on the phone. I'm leaving my flat right now ... I'll be there in a minute, okay? ... I'm turning the latch and leaving the flat ... walking down the stairs and any moment now I'll be out on the street ... are you walking?'

'Yes. I'm walking as fast as I can.'

'I'm opening the front door ... okay? I'm out on the street ... going past the curry house ... I'm just near the church ... turning down the bicycle alley ... I'm nearly there, okay ... I'm here, I'm here. Can you see me?'

And there at the end of the street was Barney, waving with one hand, his phone in the other. I ran all the way to him, as fast as I could, and he put his arms around me and assured me I was safe.

Back at the flat we drank some tea while I sat on the sofa and strummed a guitar. Barney cooked some food and hummed along with the radio. As we ate he asked about Ollie, wondering how he was coping.

'He's coping by ignoring it. He doesn't ever talk about Ecuador or being raped. I don't know if he cares really.' I replied frankly.

'Of course he cares. He's out of his depth with it all.'

'He's out of his depth? What about me? I'm going fucking insane,' I said.

'Isla, this situation is bigger than the both of you. It'll take you both over if you're not careful. It's too much for either of you to cope with.'

'He's a selfish fucking actor, that's all.'

'No he's not; he's out of his depth. Ollie's lovely. Before you went to Ecuador you loved him. Try and remember what it was you liked about him. Focus on that – not the bad points.'

Barney had always been the voice of reason. I put down the guitar and thought about Ollie, remembering his smile from the night before. A pang of guilt stung me for slating his character.

'I loved his smile,' I said, 'and the way we used to dance together. We used to love to dance, anywhere we could.'

Whenever I felt down Ollie urged me to dance, and if we couldn't afford to go out and find a dance floor, we'd dance in the flat around the living room and bounce on the bed.

'I miss dancing,' I told him. 'I miss our spontaneity. I miss my sense of fun.'

Barney counselled me as I sat in Bertha, driving through London and its stop-start traffic. We filled up the van with strangers' belongings, moving it on to their new homes; boxes full of books and trunks full of objects wrapped carefully in paper. Some people were moving on to new beginnings and others were leaving the past behind, their trinkets of sentimentality left out for the bin men.

Three weeks later Ollie's play came to a close, and finally the cast, the crew, and the young, quiet writer could relax, let go, and celebrate. A room was hired above a pub in Soho for the end-of-show party and Ollie bought some new clothes. He looked handsome and I was proud of him, but when he asked me to go with him, I didn't have the will.

'Come and dance with me,' he said. 'It'll be good for you.'

I couldn't think of anything I'd rather do less. I could go through the motions, but didn't see the point. Instead, while he was celebrating I drank wine and watched TV and wondered when the winter would finally succumb to spring. Would I be here at all if it hadn't been for the third man, I asked myself, as I smoked another pack of cigarettes?

CHAPTER THIRTEEN
THE GOBLIN

COVENT GARDEN, LONDON, ENGLAND

AUGUST 2004

Sal and I grabbed another handful of pistachio nuts and ordered more wine as we spied upon the customers. Bellini's was the venue, a Moroccan restaurant around the corner from The Exhibition, awash with colour like an African sunset on a windy day. Small wooden staircases led from the ground floor up to intimate alcoves that jutted out over the restaurant like grand theatre boxes. Every Thursday evening the alcoves filled with Opera singers who sang of love, sorrow, and retribution to the waiters and diners below. Gianni, the leading man, was large, round, and Italian with knowing brown eyes that could change from joyous to heartbroken within two beats of a bar. Unlike his voice, his hair was now wilting, and a small patch of scalp shone beneath the lights where once there had been oodles of curls. Every weekend Gianni ran a fruit stall at the famous Borough Market where food-lovers from all over the city came to buy their chillies, cheese, jams, jaggery, and bottles of salubrious wines. Gianni sang out his opera as he tended to his stall, gathering large, intrigued crowds around him who were instantly mesmerised and quietly hypnotised into buying bags full of bananas and pears.

Currently Sal and I were sitting in one of the boxes hiding from Goblin. We were at a good vantage point to observe his entrance, should he suddenly arrive. Both of us knew it was unlikely that he would, yet each of us enjoyed the pretence that he might. It added tension to the evening and heightened our laughter. Eagerly we watched the doors as we discussed the day's dramas.

Goblin had arrived at the market, uninvited, early in the morning when the traders' banter and greetings were still occupying the airwaves. Deborah had caught sight of the back of him, sidling between Graham's baked-potato stall and Helen's Henna tattoos. Clearly, like the rest of us, Goblin was a free man who could come and go as he pleased, but what set him apart from everyone else was that only four weeks ago he'd been told by Sal that she no longer wanted him to be part of her life. Yet now he was back, strutting around the market, Sal's words bouncing off him like water off a duck's down. When Deborah told Sal about the Goblin's return she'd jumped out of her seat, quicker than a cat pouncing on its prey, knocking caddies of tea from her counter, which clattered like hailstones on the shiny tiled floor.

'Bloody hell,' she said, 'I left him in France. Why the hell has he turned up here?' Sal clearly had no misgivings about her decision to leave Goblin behind.

'He's here to see you, my dear,' Deborah laughed.

'Well he can bloody well get his arse out of here. Bleedin' stalker.' Sal was adamant.

Four weeks earlier Sal had travelled to the south of France with a suitcase full of dainty shoes, well-cut clothes, and all of his stuff that was cluttering up the flat and getting on her nerves. After their parting, which was devoid of tears but fraught with temper, she walked away thinking it would be forever, and caught a train to Paris, where she wore her dainty shoes and well-cut clothes and dined in a restaurant by the Eiffel Tower. As soon as Sal returned to London, she knew that breaking up with Goblin had been the right thing to do.

'I didn't love him, Isla. And I knew I never could. It had long past its sell-by date for being a bit of fun. We stopped having sex ages ago. He felt more like a dad than a lover. And besides, who'd want to have sex with a goblin?'

Having sex with the Goblin was something I'd never imagined, but now she'd put the thought into my head it lingered in my mind in a rather awkward way until the hordes of tourists came and thankfully distracted me. Along with the sightseers came the second sighting of the hapless Frenchman. He'd been spotted in the café upstairs, overlooking the market, and though Sal was unaware of his presence, news travelled fast. Tony leaked the Goblin's whereabouts.

'Sal, isn't that French bloke you used to hang around with sitting upstairs, scoffing a plate of Chinese?' he asked.

'That's it! I'm calling the police – he's bloody stalking me! Is he thick in the head or something?'

'He's only having a Chinese. You can't call the police over that. Every man's entitled to his sweet and sour,' Tony said playfully.

'Well why doesn't he go down Chinatown, like everybody else? It's cheap crap up there – everyone knows that. And there's bleedin' mice.'

Sal grabbed her bag and hurtled out of the market shouting her orders, leaving me in charge of the shop. 'I ain't coming back until he's gone,' she said defiantly.

Deborah was allocated the role of chief spy and ran upstairs to the restaurants and cafes, wearing her glasses for clearer inspection. Jae owned the usually popular Indian café, advertising his discount meals on a board outside, but today he hadn't enticed many diners and Jae was sitting behind his tureens of biryanis and bhunas, rice, and raithas, idly stirring the dishes with a long, metal ladle, wishing he'd been born with a large, silver spoon. Next to Jae was Lloyd's stall, where Jerk Chicken and spicy patties were sold and tea was given away to the homeless. Lloyd was a huge man who used to spar with Frank Bruno but had stopped his boxing days when he'd married Greta, the youngest of Jae's three daughters. The couple had enticed many loyal customers who liked to hear Lloyd's fighting stories or be warmed by his wife's watermelon smile. The café next to Lloyd's was Goblin's current hideout, where he was presently sitting, tucking into a plate of Chinese with a white plastic fork. Half an hour later Goblin must have remembered that along with Sal's head for money came a determined, stubborn streak. He could sit on his pew, chewing sweet and sour for the rest of the night, but Sal would never return. Eventually, after a long time waiting, the Frenchman threw down his napkin and left the market through the glass double doors, defiantly flinging his tweed jacket over his shoulder. Deborah passed on the news and Sal returned, flustered and fiery, but with her resolve firmly intact. She had parted from her overseas lover and there was to be no going back on her word.

'We said our goodbyes on foreign shores, next to the sea, with boats bobbing up and down. It was romantic. A good ending to the whole thing, like a film, and he goes and spoils it all by coming down here and stuffing his face.'

That evening, as we opened another bottle of wine I asked Sal why she'd undergone such a sudden change of heart.

'You've always had two men,' I said, 'so why, after all this time, have you decided to have one?'

'For now, one's enough,' she replied evasively.

'As long as there are two men, you can always be in love with the idea of love – the choices, the drama, and the excitement of it all. But as soon as there's one, you're declaring a real love to him, and only to him ... I think you've said goodbye to Goblin because you're in love with Jimmy.' I spoke my words of wine-fuelled wisdom with a garbled lilt and a slur.

'Who are you? Miss Marple?' Sal laughed.

A troop of traditionally dressed Bavarian buskers came through the door, squeezing accordions and rattling tambourines.

'So are you?'

'Am I what?' she asked.

'In love with Jimmy?' I repeated.

'What about you?' Sal evaded the question once more.

'What about me?' I asked.

'You ain't got one man – you ain't got two. You ain't got bleedin' any. I detect a broken heart.'

'Now who's the detective?' I laughed.

'So what's going on?'

'I go on loads of dates – you know I do,' I told her. 'I just haven't met the right one yet.'

Since I'd been working at the market I'd been on numerous dates, all of which ended in disaster and were rehashed to Sal the next morning. Sal relished the scenes of embarrassment and pitied the poor men's souls. 'How have they got through life so far?' she'd say and shake her head in disbelief.

Sal's favourite oddball was a young South African who barely uttered a word throughout the whole of the dinner date. I'd worked very hard to engage him in conversation but nothing seemed to interest him. His home country was boring, his job got him by, and his personal life was fuelled neither by adventure nor tranquil days of contemplation. I gave up speaking to him and ordered more wine, hoping I could drink him away.

'Is that a courgette?' he asked, pointing at the orange vegetable on my side dish. These were the first words he'd uttered for nearly half an hour.

'No, it's a carrot,' I replied, and promptly asked for the bill.

Or there was Johnny, the estate agent, who arrived at a village pub in Highgate, fuelled on cocaine. He bought me a drink and was sick. I left through the bathroom window.

'What happened to that actor man you said you used to live with?' Sal asked, as she placed some coins in the busker's upturned tambourine.

'Who? Ollie?' I asked.

'The one who was in *Fat Friends*.'

'That's Ollie. I don't know what happened to him,' I replied. 'We lost touch with each other.' I gave an easy answer to an uneasy question.

'I think there's some unfinished business there,' Sal said.

Sal and her sixth sense were right. There were a lot of loose and frayed ends that had never been tied. Eventually Ollie and I went our separate ways. It had been difficult to end the relationship, and for months we'd lived in a vacuum of accusations, guilt, and misunderstandings. Together we felt lonely and apart we'd both found freedom. Ollie had never really understood the enormity of rape; the sickening violence or the crushing psychological after-effect, and whatever Ollie hadn't understood he had chosen to ignore. He grew tired of my despair and wanted his old girlfriend back, but my life had stopped while his had kept moving. I needed time to heal and breathe and start all over again.

Some nights I switched on the television and he appeared like a ghost caught in a transparent box. I could read his emotions instantly, before he spoke a line, and I noticed trivial details about him that I'd forgotten; his long artistic fingers or the cow's lip in the front of his hair. I even spoke to him sometimes, but he was lost in a time that came from the past and watching him made me feel hollow like a vase without flowers. And so I'd switch off the television and stare at my phone, wondering whether to call him.

'Isn't he on TV tonight? Why don't you ring him after his programme's finished?' Sal said, willing romance into my life.

'I might do ... so where do you think Goblin is?' I asked, changing the subject.

'God knows,' she replied, 'but I can't have him sniffing round my place. If Jimmy finds out I'm scuppered. He's a proud man, is Jimmy. I don't think an affair will sit well with him.'

I couldn't imagine exactly who an affair would sit well with, but I decided not to say.

'So you do want to be with Jimmy!' I declared.

Sal laughed, revealing her emotions as more wine ran out of the bottle. 'I've lived many lives in my one short lifetime: a teenage wife, a trader, a fool, and a cleaner. I bought some property in Spain and set up a new life there. I've had money and lost money, and sailed on yachts and lived with a millionaire. I wanted kids, and tried to have them, but found out I couldn't, and then I tried some more. I spent thousands on IVF and even more on clothes to keep me sane. But one thing I've learned from it all is: look at what you've got and not at what you ain't.'

I filled my glass half full. 'So why did it take you so long to get rid of Goblin?' I asked, intrigued.

'I am the queen,' she decreed, 'and queens will always have suitors. It's up to me to choose who I shall have and when.'

I smiled at Sal's self-respect. She was now totally in control of her domain, after a long uphill battle, and this time nobody would ever topple her.

The buskers left the restaurant, bowing graciously to their audience, before cascading out onto the street.

'Thank God that racket's gone,' Sal said, and she ordered some side dishes to soak up the alcohol.

'I'm sorry you couldn't have children,' I said.

'It's okay. It's all in the past. If it was meant to be, it would have happened. What about you? Do you want any?' Sal asked.

'I was pregnant once,' I said, 'but the baby was ectopic and had to be removed.'

'That's awful,' Sal said. 'Who was the father?'

'Ollie,' I replied. I remembered the hospital waiting area and daytime TV flickering in the corner of the room as a talk-show host played God. His earnest looks to camera made me feel nauseous and the cheering audience frayed my nerves. But there was nothing else to look at in the airless room, not even a window to stare out of. I had run out of places to lose myself. I drank some water from a small plastic bottle and waited for the results of tests I'd taken for any sexually transmitted diseases that the rapists might have given me. My stomach iced over as a nurse called out my name. She was older than me, kind and maternal, but I couldn't read her smile. Was she telling me the news was bad, but together we'd all pull through? Or maybe she was expressing encouragement – don't worry, we've got your results and everything's going to be fine. She opened the door to a neat, small office where a young doctor was sitting behind a Formica desk. He acknowledged me with another indecipherable smile, and an offer of a plastic chair.

'I'm Dr Cottonley. We have your results and you needn't worry, Miss Nutbrown; everything's okay. I'm afraid you will have to wait another four weeks for the results of your Aids test, but you know that already ...?'

'Yes. They told me when I arrived,' I acknowledged.

'There is one thing we have to tell you though ... You're pregnant.'

'I can't be!' I was shocked, yet I felt instantly warmed by the news.

'Have you been bleeding?'

'Yes.'

'Then I'm afraid there is some kind of abnormality with the pregnancy. You need to have a scan straight away.' The warm feeling left.

'What's wrong with it?' I asked.

'I don't know. They'll be able to give you more information after the scan,' he smiled. This time I could read his smile; it was an uneasy sympathetic one. 'I understand, Miss Nutbrown, you were raped?'

I felt embarrassed because he did. I tried to cover up his awkwardness by earnestly nodding like the host on the TV show.

'This is too much for one person to cope with,' he said. 'You need some help – I've made an appointment with the hospital's psychologist.'

At three o'clock I had an embryonic scan. 'We'll call you with the results very shortly,' said the radiographer.

At seven o'clock I walked to another wing and had an hour's session with a psychologist. He was a confident man with a graceful demeanour, dressed in a casual dark grey suit. His appearance was serious but his tone was friendly as he tried to lighten the weight of his words.

'Isla, you know there's a chance you might have Aids. How do you think you will cope if you do have the disease?'

'Life goes on,' I said. 'I suppose it'll just be a little shorter. I'll have to make sure I fit it all in a bit faster.'

He wrote down some notes on a sheet of white paper stapled to a beige cardboard file. My patient number was written on the front: 1046.

'My first stop would be The Great Wall of China,' I said, laughing at my flippancy.

He wrote more notes in 1046.

'Gallows humour,' I explained.

'So what you're ultimately saying is that you'd try and make the most out of life?' he asked.

'Yes, of course. You have to ... when faced with adversity and all that.' He scratched something into the beige file with his fountain pen.

My words were purposefully cagey. I didn't want him to put me or my scenario into a box. How I was feeling was ever-changing. Some days I found moments of peace, but other days, like that day, it felt as though a fault line was running through it and everything around me could instantly crumble. It was as though he was trying to label me and my feelings. Emotions should be released and understood, not diagnosed and analysed. To keep such intense sensations inside your body and mind is damaging and if he were helping me to release them I would see him as nurturing, but to label such feelings felt clinical and cold.

The psychologist moved on to the rapes. Did I have any reoccurring images? What was going through my mind? Could I remove myself partially from what happened because it took place in South America? What were my fears? I told him my worst fear was being raped again.

'It's unlikely to happen a second time,' he said. 'The chances are very remote – probably a one in two million chance ... if that.'

He was trying to be kind and encouraging, but his words weren't really helping. The probability of being raped by strangers in the first place was highly unlikely, yet it did happen. 'I read something in a newspaper yesterday,' I said, 'where a girl was raped on the way back from a gig and dumped in the middle of nowhere. She hailed down a passerby on a motorway for help, but instead of helping her, the bastard raped her again and left her by the side of the road. I'm sure she didn't think it would happen once in her life, never mind about twice in one night.'

'I read that too, but it's an extreme circumstance,' he replied.

'But it happened nevertheless,' I said.

'As I said, the chances of it happening again are extremely remote.'

'I know – but you asked my worst fear and I answered. And besides, the chances of being gang-raped in the first place are exceptionally rare, as I said, but I was.'

I understood the rationality behind his words, and I also realised he was trying to help, but ultimately he had no concept of how I was feeling and his statistics felt like he was pouring oil onto water. Emotions and statistics don't marry.

'I do understand what you mean,' he said, sensing my frustration. 'A few years ago I witnessed a fight in Little Venice. There was blood everywhere. It was very frightening. An image of a man with his cheek sliced and bleeding stayed with me for a long time. It took a few years for that memory to go ... it was very disturbing. Especially in such an area.'

'I don't think a fight in a pub can be compared to gang rape at gunpoint,' I said bluntly, 'whether it happened in New Cross or Little Venice. Now I'm going to play cod psychologist here. I think the fact it happened in Little Venice jolted you out of your comfort zone, more so than the fight itself.'

Little Venice was an affluent area of London built by the side of a canal where streets were lined with huge houses and people's dreams fulfilled. Nightmares didn't lurk in the shadows of Little Venice.

'It sounds as though you might have been less disturbed if it had happened in a shady area of Hackney.' Statistically, nightmares were found in Hackney.

'It was shocking and sudden and I was always on edge after it had happened – that's all I meant,' he said and then he laughed. 'Shouldn't I be asking you the questions?'

The sound of his laughter cut through the tension which had grown between us. I began to speak more openly. 'I dread it happening again, but I think about it all the time. If I'm on the tube and I'm left in the carriage with two or three men, I imagine they're going to gang up on me, and I look through the carriage doors to see if there are any women anywhere ... My boyfriend's friend's brother was raped in London and he said this was exactly how he felt. He couldn't bear ...'

'A man? The person you're referring to is a man?' the psychologist asked, cutting me off.

'Yes,' I said.

'This is terrible. Where did it happen? How long ago?' An expression of alarm crossed his face.

'It was near a tube, late at night. I can't remember where.'

'Did they catch them?'

'No, I don't think they did,' I replied.

And now finally he'd grasped the concept of my situation. He understood my anguish because suddenly he saw that rape could happen to men. It might happen to him. He had put himself momentarily in the position of a man who was innocently making his way home, when he was attacked and raped, and now he could feel his fear. Like a fight breaking out in an affluent area, he'd been abruptly removed from his comfort zone. I left him with his beige 1046 file.

The following evening I was sitting with Ollie at the kitchen table playing out a charade of normality: food simmering on the gas stove, tea brewing in the teapot, and Radio Four talking on the white chipped windowsill as condensation dripped down the panes. My mobile phone buzzed on the slats of a wooden chair next to me, where the night before Ollie's friend had been sitting. I had found his conversation tiring. I answered the call.

'Miss Nutbrown, we have the results of your scan. I'm afraid you must to come to the hospital immediately.'

I called a cab, packed a bag, and left. The taxi driver drove us through the night, the headlights of his car lighting up the rain that slanted in the wind like rainfall in a black and white film. He pulled up outside the hospital. I handed him some money, and he tipped me with good luck.

Like the streets outside, the ward was hushed as people slept, worried, and wondered. A suited consultant and his well-dressed team came to my bedside, penning me in with his words and a curtain which they whisked around my bed.

'The baby is ectopic, which means it's growing in your fallopian tube. We have to remove it.' He pushed a consent form in front of me. 'There's a very high chance you might die. It's likely to burst your tube, which will kill you.'

Just like the psychologist, he reeled out some statistics. I signed the form and chose, like Sal, to believe the baby wasn't meant to be.

As Sal and I discussed our lives in Bellini's, overlooking the lovers and tourists and milling waiters, I once again omitted the rapes. We weren't salaciously sharing revelations, like two guests on a talk show programme; we were merely talking as friends do. It wasn't that I had chosen to look at life through rose-tinted glasses, but my thoughts very rarely strayed to the mountain anymore. As I finished my story, the opera singers arrived on cue through the main door, clutching their costumes and music. Sal decided it was time for us to leave.

'I ain't looking at Gianni's bald head all night. There's enough of them down at the market.' And so we left our perches behind and headed home in the twilight.

That evening I switched on TV and watched Ollie perform, echoing the past through his actions. I thought about Sal egging me on, asking me to call him, willing love back into my life, but I switched off my phone and the lights for the night and chose, instead, not to have a care in the world.

CHAPTER FOURTEEN

HOME

YORK, ENGLAND

15 DECEMBER 1999

Bottle-green Bertha whizzed along the empty motorway. Bare winter trees stood by the roadside, swaying on the borders of fields covered by snow. Sheep huddled together with their black heads bowed, the white snow betraying their grey muddy coats. The wind blew hard across the carriageway and it took all of Barney's strength to steer Bertha straight. The radio warned of severe gales, but the storm was now behind us, London was far away, and in front was a long, open road. In the back of the van were all my belongings. Finally I'd stopped trying to overcome everything by myself. I was leaving London, knowing I needed some breathing space and someone to lighten the load. I was going back home to live with my parents. I had been hurtling towards a breakdown quicker than Bertha was careering to the North. Six months earlier Sara had left too, moving to Bristol to start a new life with Ali. She was buying a dog, she told me over the phone; a large one to protect her.

'I feel as though I need guarding after what happened in Ecuador,' Sara said.

It was the only time she had referred to the rapes since our return. Her relocation severed our friendship for good. I wished that all it would take was a big dog to make me feel safe, but since returning from Ecuador, whenever I'd found myself alone with a man I felt sick in the pit of my stomach and had found it hard to breathe. I imagined shopkeepers pulling out guns from beneath their counters and forcing me into the back where they'd rape me and kick me and shoot me dead. I saw businessmen hiding their guns in leather briefcases and the men sitting on tubes concealing their weapons in everyday sports bags. The line between my imagination and reality was beginning to blur severely.

It was while I was waiting for a friend, sitting in a cafe in a London park, that an epiphany hit me like a falling star. I'd been surveying my surroundings like an off-duty policeman. In my mind the gardens held a false sense of utopia. Deer were grazing placidly in their lush green pens, couples meandered through avenues of trees, and dogs frolicked, bounding after sticks while their owners beamed with pride. But it was all a smokescreen to a seedier world, a place where death and murder were imminent.

I peered into the undergrowth and looked through the avenue of trees: lovers kissed, a dog barked, and an elderly couple held hands, and as I looked further out into the horizon where the winter sun was setting, serene and timeless, I saw exactly the place where murderers lurked, in the recesses of my mangled subconscious. In the evening I phoned Barney and asked him to take me home.

We arrived in York at the beginning of December, on a Saturday afternoon. Barney and I unpacked my belongings from out of the van; shoes and coats, trunks of books, lamps, rugs, a guitar, an amp, and a box full of showreels with Work Stuff written on the front.

I sat on my single bed beside the pine drawers where the red wooden clock used to stand and the mouse used to sway to the beat of the tick and the tock. Finally I felt safe. As safe as the little girl who used to wonder where the mouse was running to. I had no idea how to start my life over again or where I was going, but at the moment all I cared about was the warm feeling of safety. That night the wind picked up and sleet tapped on the windowpane. The snow was unlikely to thaw for some time.

The following morning I heaved all my belongings into the cold spare room where once there'd been a bunk bed and a small wooden desk. Radio Four drifted upstairs from the kitchen, and bowls and plates clattered together as dad put them away after breakfast. As I unpacked my clothes I was surrounded by familiarity, warmth, and love, just as I had been as a child. Suddenly I remembered the white plastic Sindy wardrobe I used to play with on the bedroom floor, and curvy blonde Sindy galloping over Ohio cornfields to meet her farmhand lover boy, Ken. I had filled the plastic wardrobe with tiny clothes, shoes, and a child's imagination, and when I was bored of that, I'd pretend I was a sprite or a witch and cast spells beneath the willow tree at the bottom of the garden, or search the house for ghosts. My brother and I often heard two ghost cats mewing beneath the bunk beds whenever we slept in the spare room. We fought and laughed and ate midnight feasts and named the ghost cats 'Holly' and 'Heidi'. The same imagination I'd had as a child was now leading me to paranoia and dead-end streets where men held guns.

I wanted to protect the little girl who had played with her Sindy, with hair in bunches, oblivious to everything but the world she imagined in front of her. I wished she'd never grown up and had her innocence so violently torn from her, and I wondered what I would say to her if I could go back in time. Don't grow up ... there's too much heartache ahead. But she has to, as no one really is Peter Pan. And I wonder if hardship has made me grow, as an adult, in a spiritual way perhaps. But I don't think abuse helps anyone grow. I think it hurts, and some people heal while some people don't. If I really could go back in time, I think to myself, I'd tell the little girl playing with Sindy, Don't go up to Mount Mojanda. One spring day you will have a choice in your life to take a path up a mountain. Don't go. Stay in the hostel. Stay safe in Otovalo. And I wonder what would have happened if I hadn't taken the path, and a parallel life unfolds before me. A life where I'm still acting and laughing and joining in with friends, not a place where I'm trapped, fearful, and lost. And the feeling reminds me of being bullied at school, but somehow I overcame the hardship when I was a little girl. Perhaps I should ask the small child playing with the doll what she would do to conquer such intense emotions and dread. The child had clarity and the ability to wonder, but the adult does not.

My mind begins to spin. I'm sitting on the bed as the wooden mouse tick-tocks next to me, wondering why I have to go to school every single day. It feels like a prison. I'm being bullied, I need to escape, but each morning there's no choice but to put on my brown school uniform and walk to school where the day begins in a room with a piano and an empty grate, where once a fire would have roared in a Victorian grand terraced house. Fifty bewildered children sit around me and a religious lesson follows; a prayer and then a hymn. Mystified, we all file into different classrooms and soon the bullying begins. By the teachers, though – not the pupils, and none of us knows why.

The school is a throwback to Victorian times in ethos as well as architecture. The red-bricked terraced house has a small stone yard where pieces of sharp broken bottles are cemented to the top of it so no one can break in and climb over its walls. But in my eyes it seems as though the glass is there so no one can get out. There is a cold, dark outside toilet too, in the yard, where spiders hide in cracks. At dinner time, an old woman dishes out food from large vats in the tiled old-fashioned kitchen and shoves it on our desks beneath our small noses. It is usually vile and inedible, but if we haven't eaten it by the end of the dinner hour the cooking's brought back out again, after the bell has rung for home time, and the mess on the plate is forced down our pursed little mouths.

One small, sensitive boy, Benjamin, cries like a waterfall as he plays with the limp mound of lettuce on his course cream dinner plate. Snot streams from his nose onto his food like an endless squirt of putrid salad cream, but he's forced to eat it – there's no way out – and he fights and squirms and vomits. His anguish distresses all the other children and we feel every forkful he eats. Later that day he's made to eat what he left on his plate. All we can think of is cold snot and puke.

And every day I come back home feeling downhearted and fretful. School is the only reality I've experienced apart from my home. Is this how life will always be? But I got through it. I found a way of coping, and now I'm wracking my brains to remember what the little girl did to cope.

And suddenly I remember the magic feeling of entering the wardrobe and the woods of Narnia. The little girl with the Sindy escaped her fraught world by burying herself in the pages of books. There were far more enticing places to visit where fauns talked and lions walked and queens cast spells of ice. And presently, as an adult, I watch the snow fall outside, soft and silent like ghosts, and the scene brings to mind my favourite poem, *Walking Through the Woods on a Snowy Evening*. I loved it as a child and learned it off by heart.

I spent the following morning hunting for my first edition of *The Lion the Witch and the Wardrobe*, and searching for my favourite poem in amongst the books of poetry sitting on the bookshelf in the corner of my room. I opened the window for some air and stared at the long garden where the willow swayed at the far end, like Salome enchanting King Herod. The snow fell from her branches onto the ground below where two pet cats were buried and a small rabbit I'd named 'Munchie'. I remember one summer when dad and I built his hutch from chicken wire and planks of timber wood while we waited for him to be born at a farm nearby. He arrived one day, black, white, and small and I fed him some toast and he slept in some hay. Twenty years later dad was helping me rebuild my life again using the same tool he had used back then, his unconditional love.

But with every step forward there are two steps back, and not long after arriving in York I received an email from Maria explaining she was stopping her investigation and closing the case. There wasn't any point, she explained, in paying her anymore because the bastards will never be found. 'Good luck' were the words she signed out with and I wondered if there was such a thing as luck, and if so, is it ever good?

And that all too familiar feeling of things going wrong came back to me – a feeling known as despair. Like the snow around me I'd forgotten what the world would look like without it. Injustice prevailed and the rapists were free men and no doubt always would be. I pictured Maria once more, pleading with me to have them killed, frantically pacing the office, her hair curly and wild like cusps of crashing waves, her words passionate and adamant. But my conscience, a coward or a saint, had made its decision.

And I hear myself, once again, pleading to the third man's conscience: Walk away, rise above it, and walk away.

And I've returned to Mount Mojanda where I'm lying on my back. The khaki grass is rough and green. I feel it on the side of my face as I turn my head towards the attackers. I can see beneath the blindfold. Limited vision, a small keyhole to my fate. I watch the third man's white trainers shuffle. There's mud on the side of them, seeping into worn, cracked leather. Will he walk away? Will he save my life? Is he a coward or a saint? One foot stubs out a cigarette end, and both feet turn towards me. I prepare to be raped, gagging again in my gag. He's standing right by me. I feel a light, soft material on my bare legs. I try and raise my head to see what it is as the wind picks up. The trainers have gone and the voices are trailing away. The tyres of their sky blue pickup truck crunch on gravel and the sound of the accelerating engine fades into the distance. I am safe. His conscience has saved me. He did the right thing. I did the right thing, I tell myself, by sparing their lives. And even if I didn't, it's too late now.

The computer is bright in the dimly lit dining room but the light outside is fading and the winter sun is low in the sky. The email stares at me unblinking. I did what I had to, I tell myself again, and try and stop my whirring thoughts. Dad laughs in the room next door. Humanity is restored.

The same evening I picked up my guitar. Its strings were dusty from lack of use, but all I could write were melancholy songs about the third man and I quickly tired of putting myself in his muddy white shoes. I found a pen instead and began to write, just as I had done as a little girl. A short story began to unfold – a magical tale set on a boat. It began to lift my spirits and took me away from the dark place I'd come from during my last few months in London, where the city had become lonely and cold with no one to relate to. But I'd purposefully chosen solitude as I could no longer bear the effort of talking to people I couldn't relate to. Like a person living in a foreign land, unable to speak the language, communicating became too wearing, so I shut down and dreamed of home. And the loneliness became a burdensome friend who never left me alone. It was always there in my mind and even if I asked it to leave, it wouldn't, but instead it spoke to me constantly. I asked it why it was there, and wondered whether 'normal' people had a lonely friend and so I looked around at the normal people and wondered what their natural lives involved. But whatever they were doing seemed alien to me – mothers pushing prams, cooing to their babies, and talking with their toddlers. In pubs and cafes people talked of work and in restaurants they laughed in large groups. You're strange, my lonely friend told me. That's why I talk to you, because you're extremely strange and you no longer know what reality is and what reality isn't. And my friend was right. I began to disconnect from people more and more and soon I felt like I didn't have any control over anything, like the little girl who dreaded another day at school.

Feeling frightened, feeling scared. Tomorrow there's more of the same. Benjamin's dumplings get brought out again in a Victorian school that feels like a prison, where the headmistress is old and looks like a witch. Her hair is grey and curly and she wears an old-fashioned dress that trails on the floor. She is a figurehead – the owner of the school – but is too old to teach, so instead she makes demands from her parlour upstairs. I sense the teachers don't like her, the same way they don't like us. She has so many wrinkles – they look like the white pithy stuff that covers the flesh of a peeled tangerine. I wonder if all the uneaten dumplings at dinner time sit beside her in her parlour and together they make one big stew of bitterness. I also wonder, if you picked away at her wrinkles like you pick away at the pithy stuff, would you find someone sweeter who hadn't been eaten up by life? A young girl that laughs and smiles like we do when the teachers' backs are turned?

Presently, as an adult, I look back at Tangerine and wonder if she'd had a difficult life and that's why she ended up so bitter. Fuck. What if I end up as sour-tasting as her? And instantly I'm sad because the helplessness I feel isn't my own fault. Like the teachers at school, I was vulnerable and at the whim of someone else's power. And they walked free at the end of the day, just like the rapists, and I am left in my prison. I feel so angry, I'm so fucking sick of people, and I pick up the bedside lamp in my room, a pink art deco lamp with a glass round shade, and I imagine the lamp is one of the rapists' heads and I hurl it as hard as I can against the wall. I pick up a hairbrush and smash it down on the dressing table over and over again. The wood on the dresser dents and I wish it was their fucking cortex, being crushed with every whack. Anger careers through me as I think that my whole life has been in vain. What's been the point of it all when I end up at twenty-seven worse off than the child I used to be? At least, as a child, I wasn't afraid to walk down a street. What was the point of learning to act, learning to love, learning to walk, when it's all been fucking thwarted? And the intense feelings make me well up and cry and I sit on the floor amongst the shards of glass and remember the little girl playing with her Sindy and I try to pick up the pieces around me. I think of the Sindy picnics I used to have, when she sat with Ken and together they drank out of plastic beakers the size of peas. But my mind reverts back to the picnic by the Lakes Mojanda where Sara and I ate olives and bread, tomatoes and cheese, and the sky in front of us was endless and blue. Travels, adventures, and the whole of our lives were ahead of us, for two hours more. And then my freedom disappeared, and now I'm in a prison and the rapists are free.

And I wonder what they're doing now with their free time ... sitting in a bar with a couple of friends playing cards across the table, driving over the Andes beneath a moon, watching TV, shooting the breeze, or betting on horses, dogs, or flies? And here I am, frightened to walk down a street. And I wonder if they ever think about me, and this thought connects me so closely to them that I instantly feel nauseous. The possibility I might wander into their minds sickens me. I've been trying to battle them and keep them away from me, but what if I'm inside their heads when they're daydreaming or sexually frustrated?

But I can no longer think like this – it's leading me nowhere and I've experienced too much to put myself through it again. All I wish for now is to walk down a street without feeling scared, without the thought that a man with a gun will suddenly appear from nowhere and shoot me point blank dead. Now is a time to ignore the past. Now is a time to heal. The rapists are free and the case is closed and I have to try and bury it away in my psyche somewhere. I know I'll find it all again someday, but how it will appear to me, as yet I don't know. A chronic drink problem, talking to imaginary friends on lonely park benches, prescription drugs or a long walk with God, but for now I have to let go and hand myself over to trust again.

And I ask the little girl what she would do now and she decides I should sit at the dining room old oak table and carry on writing the short story I'd started – magic and narrow boats in France. And so I carry on in longhand in a brand new pad. The smell of new paper and the feeling of it, smooth on my palms, bring me a feeling of happiness. A new reality unfolds on the sheets as a mysterious man teaches spells to a woman from England. Benita is her name. She is young and fiery and strong. This world is far more enchanting than my reality.

I glance up at the window. It is dark now outside, but I can just make out the willow at the bottom of the garden, and I remember the spells I used to cast beneath its drooping branches when I was a girl, and I think of the cats and the small black and white rabbit buried there. I was devastated when they died; the rabbit passed away first. A loud knock on the front door woke me one morning. Standing in the doorway was our next-door neighbour, wearing old, dishevelled gardening clothes and an expression as solemn as a sermon. A young domestic rabbit had been found on a patch of short-mown grass, lying on its side, three gardens down. It was black and white and small. He'd eaten some poison. I had cried and sobbed and felt utterly heartbroken and thought I'd never get used to him not being there. We got rid of the hutch and his chicken wire run and waited for the sadness to lift. And eventually it did. Somehow I thought about him less and less, and time did indeed heal all wounds. One day, all this sadness I have inside me now and all the thoughts about the rapists will fade, like the sun in winter fades – hazy and mellow – it's gone. Like Munchie faded beneath the soil. This will all fade one day. This time will pass.

CHAPTER FIFTEEN
WALKING IN THE WOODS

LLANGOLLEN, WALES.

29 APRIL 2000

> Whose woods these are I think I know,
> His house is in the village though
> He will not see me stopping here
> To watch his woods fill up with snow.
>
> My little horse must think it queer
> To stop without a farmhouse near,
> Between the woods and frozen lake
> The darkest evening of the year.
>
> He gives his harness bells a shake

To ask if there is some mistake
The only other sounds the sweep,
Of easy wind and downy flake.

The woods are lovely, dark and deep
But I have promises to keep,
And miles to go before I sleep,
And miles to go before I sleep.

As the weeks passed I threw myself into my writing and immersed myself into a world of magical fiction. I filled my mind with Benita's story, pushing the rapists and gunmen away. Every morning I sat down with a mug of tea and a pen and wrote at the old oak table, overlooking the long green lawn, and soon Benita's world flourished. Characters developed as her friends arrived amongst the pages, and landscapes were painted with castles and rivers and vast, craggy hillsides. Benita and her gypsy lover became as real to me as the willow tree at the end of the garden. I could almost feel the dusty glass bottles that she poured her magical potions into. And as I carried on writing, magic began to fill my own psyche and the days began to have a softer edge. Benita's ability to believe that anything was possible began to seep into my own subconscious and gradually I too began to revel in wonder again. And the wonder came in simple forms. Meals cooked by friends, a cup of coffee in a café outdoors, a local pub quiz, a gig, and even occasionally talking to strangers. Engaging in life again was the wonder, and the lonely voice in London, who had become my burdensome friend, was now merely a distant relative. I knew it was there, but it was quieter now, and became even more distant as I started to connect with people again. A slight shift in my perception had taken place and life began to have intrigue once more. The world had spun on its axis and finally winter was giving way to spring.

And as I began to feel more hopeful I started to test myself, urging myself on, determined to overcome a nightmare. I needed to walk in a remote area again, just as Mount Mojanda had been. I had tried to once already, in mid-December, with my brother, Paul, near his home on the Welsh borders. We'd taken a walk in the woods, but I'd frozen in the midst of the trees when a fox leaped through the undergrowth. The suddenness of the noise had knotted my heart and my knees weakened beneath me like a building falling in an earthquake. So instant was my vulnerability, I had clung to Paul like a child, just as I had with Sara on the road back from Mount Mojanda. But now that trust was becoming part of me again, like the blood which ran through my veins, I decided to take another walk in the woods and swiftly called my brother.

I arrive in Wales two days later at a small village train station that has won an award for its floral display. The name of the village is displayed in a flower bed made from red and purple pansies. Paul and his girlfriend, Rose, live in a smallholding with chickens and outhouses and a large field where Rose's friend occasionally lives in a yurt. We watch a film in the evening, about a boxer, all of us sitting in front of the fire, and Rose opens some wine. I sleep in the spare room and watch the stars sparkle. They are bright and clear. We are far away from light pollution.

In the morning we walk through furrowed fields and cross a racecourse, now deserted, that leads to the dense, dark woods where a stream runs through. The rushing water echoes through the valley and we trample on uneven soil scattered with molehills. My brother is tall and dark, with thick hair that reaches the nape of his neck. He puts his arm around Rose, who is as down to earth as the soil we walk on, and has a kind and pretty nineteen-fifties face. Today she has a lilac scarf tied around her long brown hair.

For Paul and Rose it is just another Saturday, but for me it is a fresh spring day with an air of excitement. Ziggy, their black and white sheep dog, sniffs along the ground as he follows trails and scents. I watch the wood unfold around me and listen to it breathe. It is deep, dark, and enchanting with slivers of sunlight falling through bare branches and bundles of crows' nests. My fear, like the snow, which had once – not long ago – lain deep in the woods, is gradually seeping away.

Together we talk about tomorrow's adventures in the ancient town of Llangollen. A festival is taking place. Rose tells me there are arts and crafts in the old town hall and music in a marquee, but she's most excited by the tarot card reader who predicted last year that my brother would come into her life and they would live on a small working farm. My spirits are lifted. Things to do are a novelty for me, as all I'd thought about in London were people and places to avoid.

Gradually the wood becomes less dense and rays of sunshine flood through the trees, lighting the path still covered by soft, damp autumn leaves. We have reached the end of our rambling, the undergrowth wanes, and a clearing appears before us. Opposite the glade is a pub with benches and tables outside. We are all tingling from the fresh air and exercise and Rose's lilac scarf has slipped out of place. Soft drinks are bought to quench our thirst, but our good intentions leave us when we order our first pint. Three hours later we call a taxi and I fall asleep smiling.

And I think of my brother as I fall asleep and thank the heavens for him and the lifeline he has thrown me. Just by being him. In London I had been unable to function, like a fish thrown unceremoniously back into the river with a hole in its mouth, but Paul has cast me a different line that pulls me gently along with him, helping me go with the flow. Like the stream in the woods, our friendship has its natural lore, born from a lifetime spent together, and the current between us drifts the same way. I start to believe that life might no longer hurt me.

The following morning I woke feeling as light as the wind that gently blew around the outhouses. I walked over to the window with my bare feet; the floorboards felt warm where shards of sunshine had crept through the curtains. Outside, a large tabby cat crouched behind an old iron water pump, waiting to pounce on a chicken obliviously pecking at some grain on the ground. Downstairs Rose was talking to her dog as he wandered through the kitchen, his claws tapping on the old tiled floor. I wondered if I had enough money to see the tarot card reader today. Financially I was rather poor, but now I had contentment, and that was rich enough for me.

We ate breakfast at the table and jumped into a blue battered estate car which smelled of weed and oil. Ziggy sat in the back on a blanket full of dog hairs and panted excitedly as the lush green hills whizzed by. The sky looked majestic, charging our moods with excitement.

Llangollen is in the well of a valley, with a steam train and waterfalls and a river running through it. High above the town is a castle, built on a rocky hill, where legend says the Holy Grail once lived but the only inhabitants left now are crows, who stalk through the ruins like beady centurions. The river's current was strong beneath us as we walked over the ancient stone bridge. Paul and I stopped to watch the water gurgle and sing, our inner worlds both sharing the peace it brought us, but Rose didn't have the patience to pause and listen; she was excited about the tarot card reader and spurred us on through the town to find him. We weaved our way through day trippers and brightly coloured stalls assembled across the cobbled streets and pitched along the river bank where we found the man who told the future inside The Winstay pub, drinking tea from a china cup. His left hand was adorned with rings sparkling on every finger.

In the end I decided not to have a reading with Leo, even though I was curious. It wasn't because I doubted his gifts, but because the future would inevitably happen, whatever he told me, and for now I was happy in the knowledge that it would, and thankful that a trigger hadn't been pulled on the top of Mount Mojanda.

> The woods are lovely, dark and deep,
> But I have promises to keep,
> And miles to go before I sleep,
> And miles to go before I sleep.

CHAPTER SIXTEEN
BURNING THE MAN

THE GREEN GATHERING, YORKSHIRE, ENGLAND
AUGUST 2000

Spring faded and summer blazed across the country. Buskers and painters arrived in York, laying out their caps and setting up their easels by the steps of the Minster. Tourists' smiles were enigmatically captured as well as their bundles of Euros. The city bustled with life as the sun rose higher in the sky.

Rose called again from Wales inviting me to a three-day festival in Yorkshire, the Northern Green Gathering. The event was an annual affair that spiritually celebrated the earth and raised awareness to protect it.

The following week, Paul and Rose pulled up at Pontefract station in their battered blue estate car. United again, we listened to the radio with the doors open wide, waiting for my friend Kate to arrive on the next train from London. The day was glorious, the sun shone in clear blue skies, and as we walked through the site with our rucksacks on our backs, Rose's face beamed. The gathering was a myriad of tarot readers and healers sharing their knowledge and freeing their spirits in marquees, tepees, and yurts. As we put up our tents the sunlight warmed our backs and during the evening we listened to bands playing on stages powered by the wind. Our bodies danced in sauna air.

I felt the most relaxed I'd ever been since returning from Ecuador. Here, at the festival, I was amongst people who didn't want to fit in neatly with the rest of society. I'd never led a conventional life, but being a raped girl was a social taboo too far, and I'd stood on my own as an outsider. But here, with those who'd chosen to live an alternative life, I felt at home again. To be different was embraced. That night we fell asleep to the sound of campfires crackling and the strum of acoustic guitars.

The following morning, as the smell of cooked breakfasts filled the camp, the sun shone brightly, defying the occasional cloud. We leafed through the festival programme searching for entertainment, and found it in abundance – music, comedy, and theatre, workshops in craft-making, courses on yurt-building, and meetings with angels, spirit guides, and ghosts. The camp was our oyster. Traditionally the day was known as 'Llamas' – an ancient, pagan day of celebration when Gods were asked to bless the autumn with golden crops, fertile fields, and store rooms full of apples. My brother chose a Druid activity for the day, feeling a strong surge of affinity with the earth, and agreed to help build a forty-foot Wicca man, along with other bear-chested men who drank ale out of tankards strapped to their belts. Kate and Rose were happy to meander and wander the camp, while I ventured into the peace garden, stepping into a felt-covered yurt to learn a healing technique called 'Reiki'. I was intrigued, and as the teacher was offering his knowledge for a small donation only, I decided not to look a discount therapist in the heart, and spent the next four hours with Ray, a Reiki Master, covered in piercings and doused in good will.

I sat in a circle with Ray and four other pupils on bales of hay and we bonded over tea served in small Japanese cups. The yurt was cool inside and incense burned in little clay pots, swirling through the air like dancing ghosts. A sense of calm descended upon us and a dreamy atmosphere prevailed, like a pagan's dream had entered the space and left behind another reality.

Reiki, I found, isn't something you learn, but instead, a person becomes attuned to it. How it works is subjective, as most improvable things in life are. Some people say it takes a leap of faith to believe in its beneficial powers, others think it's a natural healing energy already present in nature, there are those who call it unconditional love, and there are the cynics who say it's all nonsense. Yet whatever lies behind Reiki, be it practical, esoteric, or transcendental, I enjoyed my afternoon becoming attuned, and before we all parted ways venturing out into the mellowing sun,

Ray gave us some last words of advice. The energy we'd received might unblock some unresolved emotional issues – there may be a few tears before bedtime. 'If it gets too much, come and find me. I'll be by the Wicca man,' he offered, and rolled a cigarette before stepping out of his yurt to wander through the makeshift lanes of marquees, huts, tepees, and tea tents towards the huge effigy that had now been raised upright, his arms reaching towards the honey sun. Soon he'd be blazing, set on fire, while people danced round his glow, celebrating the joy of a new season.

I found my friends back at the campsite, building fires for the evening, bustling around with logs and grates, raw sausages, and huge baking potatoes, as children played, hiding in tents while mothers laughed and cursed, foraging in rucksacks for wash bags and folded clean clothes. Reefers were rolled, fires were lit, and the sound of bongos echoed round the camp. Suddenly, as twilight fell and the sky turned crimson, an overwhelming sense of melancholy ran through me, as though I were sitting alone in an overgrown graveyard, surrounded by the tombs of soldiers. In one solitary moment, the futility of life overwhelmed me – its fleetingness, the struggles in vain, the absurdity that one day everyone here would no longer exist, and the investments of love, which in the future, like each of us, would all turn to dust. Adversity, the battles that are fought, the heartache we feel, the pain that people cause each other, and the conflict people inflict.

I wandered from the camp and found an empty field where I sat down and cried and sobbed from the pit of my stomach. I cried at the rapists' cruelty, people's indifference to violence and rape, the lack of vitriol expressed by others regarding the rapes, and the lack of comforting words of empathy or sympathy. All this negativity which had been bestowed upon me, resulted in my self-worth being shattered, and the men and women who had chosen to show such little compassion had taken part in the cowardly act of lowering my self-esteem. And I hadn't realised that I deserved any praise, because I didn't feel worthy of anything. Praise is something actors receive after a performance; it isn't a reward that rape survivors have bestowed upon them. And so, I had not been the heroine of my own story – how could I be? I'd been made to feel worthless. I didn't deserve admiration. Suddenly, I realised for the very first time that I'd given away the title of hero to somebody else, because I didn't feel justified to have it. The third man was the hero of my story. I had bestowed upon him gratitude and honour, when I should have been praising myself. I'd given him all the glory because no one had made me feel glorious. The third man had been my saviour, when the reality was I'd saved myself. And all this time I'd been thinking about him, spending my time wondering what might have happened if he'd raped me too; thanking him, somehow, for being respectful. Now I realised that he hadn't been respectful in any fucking way. He had willingly taken part in robbery, violence, and rape. The man was vile, pathetic, and weak and I hated him. I carried on crying for what seemed like hours, but the field was neither filled with blades of grass like knives, nor men force-feeding me worms, or rapists with guns. The meadow was lush and green and alive with yellow dandelions and dock leaves and butterflies the colour of lemons. I waited for the sobbing to cease, and as the night fell and bronze moths replaced the butterflies, calm prevailed and my perception had shifted as the moon had risen. The Wicca man burned on the horizon, orange and violet. A cheer went up as the flames grew higher and I raised the third man to the ground.

When I returned to camp the food was crisp and smelled delicious. As Rose filled our glasses with her homemade red wine and Kate handed out plates, I felt as happy and luscious as the cooking tasted.

The opposite of melancholy is joy, and the other extreme of futility is wonder, and as we're only here for a small, brief time, shouldn't we fill it with awe and delight? And I looked at the people around me: Paul proudly sipping his ale from his newly acquired tankard, my oldest friend Kate with Rose discussing their food and the night's bands and brownie cakes. Children laughing and mothers cursing and life around me as it should be, as it always has been, and as it always will be for generations to come. And finally I'd found some freedom. The rush of being alive.

I walked home from York station, after my weekend at the Gathering, through empty streets, twilight, and the birds' evensong. I passed the theatre where as a child I'd fallen in love with acting, and as a teenager I'd fallen head over heels with the actors. I walked past my brother's grand old school, 'AD 1047' proudly painted on its sign, and I carried on sauntering down tree-lined streets, alongside a clearing where gypsies used to graze their horses and build fires which warmed their kin. And as I finally joined the road which led to my parents' house, I realised with great joy that I'd walked home alone, and not once had I thought that a man with a gun would jump out and shoot me point blank dead.

CHAPTER SEVENTEEN
MOVING ON

CAMDEN TOWN, LONDON, ENGLAND

DECEMBER 2000

The autumn swept in golden leaves, harvest festivals, and orange grimacing pumpkins. It also brought a phone call from Carl, my old friend, the part-time drug dealer and full-time book-pusher. He called me to ask if I would run his market stall for him through the winter while he escaped the cold to follow his heart and travel around Asia. His stall was at Camden Market.

'I'll make it worth your while,' he said.

I remembered Camden being like a second home to me, with its narrow canal brimming with boats and its banks overflowing with bohemia. I recalled happy afternoons rummaging through boxes of second-hand books and rifling through racks of vintage clothes. As my imagination was no longer filled with crazed gunmen stalking the streets, I thought it would be a good idea to leave my comfort zone in York for a while and immerse myself amongst people and diversity again; to be back in a city which I had once loved. Camden seemed the perfect place to spend some time, so I quickly called Carl and agreed to run his stall. I packed a couple of bags, said a tearful goodbye to my parents, and found myself at Camden Market three days later, having found a room to rent in a house with a friend.

The stall was small and draped in silk, like a travelling puppet theatre, nestled between a young man who travelled from Wales each weekend to sell loaves of lavender soap, and a Hungarian woman selling patchwork bags and purses. Carl was overjoyed to be travelling again, and his smile was as bright as his lamps as he introduced me to some of the traders. The next day he flew to Bangkok and I was left with his stock, a pair of thermal gloves, and a large felt money belt with a goodbye good-luck note tucked inside one of its pockets. The air was filled with the smell of the food stalls; onions roasting, garlic sizzling, and curries simmering while the atmosphere bubbled with excitement. The stall holders were looking forward to Christmas, their busiest time of the year.

As the weekends passed, I formed a happy friendship with Mary, who sold children's toys, but I found a lifelong friend in Josh, a musician, who, like me, was running a friend's stall while they travelled the world.

Josh was the embodiment of free thinking, having been brought up in a seventies commune, near Liverpool, in a small town called Skem. His father had been a seventies pop star, wearing cravats and Breton tops, dancing wistfully on Top of the Pops, brandishing an accordion and a huge pair of false eyelashes. Josh's mother was now a therapist. Whether she'd become the latter because her husband had been the former was something I always wondered, but both were gentle and open-minded and had devoted their time in the seventies to a utopian way of life. Josh's background intrigued me and every weekend I learned a little more about it as I sat with him in the mornings before the bustle of the day began, drinking coffee, trying to keep warm. Josh was one of the lucky ones; he had a stall inside, in a huge converted stable, away from the rain and the wind that rustled through the leaves like a prelude to snow.

That year the winter was unforgiving. The canal-side mist didn't clear until the afternoon and other times it stayed all day, melting into the darkness that filled the sky at four o'clock. But the season brought warm scarves and bright woollen hats, mulled wine and smiles on traders' faces. Christmas gifts were bought in abundance and their pockets were lined with security.

The festive season came and went and Carl returned to spend his profits. He was now back behind his stall, tanned but cold and he quickly got colder. The Thai beach smile that he returned with rapidly turned into a scowl, as fixed as the icicles that hung from the trees. Carl couldn't afford an assistant anymore, so I had to look for another source of income and at the same time so did

Josh. Together we created a formidable plan, devising a stall like no other; an edible product that would take Camden by storm: nachos. Good, old-fashioned, dipping corn; small triangles of maize delight, served with ladles full of salsa. We celebrated our entrepreneurial creation one night in a pub by Camden Loch and drank away any niggling doubts. In retrospect, we really ought to have listened to them.

The evening before our launch we made the salsa, finely chopping bundles of coriander, slicing green chillies and pouring on platefuls of diced tomatoes. Our excitement was uncontainable. The next day we made our debut on a wooden stall in freezing cold temperatures and spent the day huddled around our neighbour's gas rings. Our sales totalled six plates of nachos, two of which were sold at half price. By the end of the day our spirits, like our food, had grown soggy, but we refused to be defeated and arrived the next week with a secret weapon: hot cheese sauce. Despite our ammunition, our bite-sized chips couldn't compete with the warmth that a bowl of curry could give. Traders observed and pitied us from afar. Marco, an Italian who sold corn on the cobs, eventually came over to give us advice. He arrived with gusto, his manner as flamboyant as his clothes.

'It's a good idea, the nachos,' he told us with kindness in a strong Italian accent. 'Keep at it, but keep changing. Try out new things. Why not buy something that will keep the nachos hot? Make it stand out – buy a machine. Instead of a popcorn-maker buy a nacho maker; big and bright, which cuts the maize into triangles and churns out the chips in front of the customer. It would be incredible.'

Josh and I exchanged playful glances. Marco's enthusiasm was infectious but both of us believed that such a machine probably only existed in his mind.

'Be careful,' Marco warned us dramatically, 'the market is always in control of you. Quickly you become its slave. It takes over your life and eats away your soul.'

Fortunately, as we were about to embark on our third weekend of unmitigated disaster, a weekend when a market was about to eat our very being but nobody would eat our product, Carl offered me a part-time job working for his friend, Will, the supplier of Carl's lampshades. This lively entrepreneur had a stall at Covent Garden Market, by the cobbled piazza, selling goods that had been slightly damaged in his warehouse.

'Same tat as mine, but just a little tear here and there,' Carl explained.

Two days later, I stepped out of the Underground into the quiet January streets, and unknowingly at the time, into a new life – a time that would bring warmth and trust, healing and camaraderie, laughter and belonging. A glorious feeling would be created at this market; the feeling of excitement, the relief of joy, and the peace found in knowing I was safe again.

The day was unusually warm for January and Covent Garden was vibrant as usual. Carmen echoed round the piazza – a pretty young opera student singing her repertoire. Tourists gathered round while she busked, while others sat at tables laughing and talking enthusiastically, their ice creams melting in the mild winter sun. I found The Exhibition Market and weaved my way through its stalls to Will's stall, which was covered by throws. A woman with shiny blond hair and a walk as confident as her smile came over and introduced herself.

'I'm Sal,' she said, 'I own the tea shop opposite. You're early ain't ya? The market doesn't get going till ten. I'd have a lie-in tomorrow if I were you. Fancy a tea?' She walked a couple of paces down the aisle, then stopped and turned around dramatically. Her hair swished, right on cue. 'By the way, don't buy anything from Graham on baked potatoes. He doesn't wash his hands after he's been to the toilet.'

The woman with the strong London accent made her way to the café, leaving me with a strange image of potatoes and toilet basins whirling around my mind. I wondered how she actually knew he didn't wash his hands. Whatever the reason, I laughed at her frankness and began to uncover my stall.

CHAPTER EIGHTEEN
TIME DID PASS

COVENT GARDEN, LONDON, ENGLAND

SEPTEMBER 2008

Sal perched on a stool in the corner of her shop. The counter had been repainted in a deep bottle green, matching the shelves lit by spotlights. Behind her, a rosy-cheeked fifties housewife dressed in a gingham skirt smiled down from a Linton's Tea poster. A pair of trousers lay on top of the counter and Sal began to stitch through the thick material with a large needle and thread. She was absorbed in her task, and swayed her head gently from side to side in time with the music playing through the tinny tannoy speakers. The shop felt snug and warm in contrast to the autumn raindrops falling on the delivery vans on the side street outside. A German family were burrowing through a basket of fruit-flavoured teas.

I squeezed my way through their bustle and bags, which they carried on their backs like shells.

'Hello stranger,' she said smiling. 'We haven't seen you round here for a while. How are you?'

'I'm good, I'm fine. How are you? Whose are the trousers?'

'Whose do you think? – Marcus's. Muggins here got lumbered with them this morning. The hems are too long.'

And as we chatted, the time and distance between us gradually cleared, like the dust on the streets outside being washed away by the rain.

'It's been bloody hard today,' Sal said. 'Well, they have.' And she nodded towards the German family, but they referring to all customers in general. 'I've had forged twenties, women with too much perfume, and Philipus banging on about his holidays. I'm exhausted and it's only one o'clock.'

There was a pause as Sal remembered her day. She shook her head in disbelief and quickly moved the conversation on. 'Fancy a tea?' she asked

'I'd love one.'

'Go and say hello to Marcus – he'd love to see you. He's got a bloody face on him today.'

I crossed over the aisle and found Marcus sitting on his tall wooden stool, immaculately dressed in a thick woollen jumper with a brown scarf and corduroy cap, like a beatnik writer.

'Isla! Isla! Where have you been?' He kissed me on each cheek. 'It's boring here now. There's no one to play with since you've gone. The man sat in your stall has a long face all day. I don't like looking at him.'

I poked my head through the lace tablecloths to catch a glimpse of the stall-holder trading from the pitch where I'd once sat and read, chattered, and drank. The man was in his mid-fifties with white wispy hair and a smart striped jacket. Contrary to Marcus's opinion, he didn't have a long, miserable face, but a small angular one with a delicate mouth and blue eyes. His wares were displayed immaculately; small, hand-painted pictures of cats in twilight pinned onto neat velvet notice boards.

'He looks nice,' I said, 'perhaps not the type to crack open the vodka at eleven in the morning, but he certainly doesn't look miserable.'

Marcus dismissed him with a wave of his hand.

'Has he been here since I left?'

'Yes, unfortunately.'

I stopped working at The Exhibition Market when Will packed up his stall for good and moved his wears to a shop in Notting Hill. Carl, whom he also employed, eventually moved to Thailand. The long, cold winters had frozen his humour and the high rents had burned holes in his pockets.

'How's business?' I asked Marcus.

'Let's not talk about such things,' he instantly replied. 'It's boring.'

'How's love?'

Marcus's dark oval eyes instantly lit up. 'I have a boyfriend.

In the end I'd spent too much time on my own. I met him, I liked him, and I needed the company. But now ...'

'Now he's boring?' I guessed. He picked off some fluff from his toilet roll holder and straightened it out. Marcus sighed. 'What does he do?' I asked.

'He's a lawyer ... solicitor ... something like that. We sit around with his friends talking about this and that – boring things. Things I don't care about.'

'I can't really imagine you hanging around with solicitors,' I said.

But Marcus had a twinkle in his eye as bright as the buttons on his teddy bears. 'I have met someone else,' he said dramatically, as though he were giving evidence to a judge.

'Really! What's he like?'

'He's absolutely beautiful. Dark, Iranian. Brown eyes, black hair. He works hard – not a person who sits around doing nothing, and he's so sweet too. He's a little bit naive – you know what I mean? He's never drunk a cocktail in his life! I don't want a man who does the drink and the drugs.'

'Like you, you mean?' I teased him.

'Exactly! Imagine another me! The mood up and down, the money here and there; it would be awful!'

'So what's the catch?' I said warily.

'The catch is: he's straight.'

'Oh God, not again.'

Marcus laughed. 'I know who you're thinking about. You're

thinking about that Spanish boy,' he said.

'I most certainly am.'

And suddenly I was lost again in dark starlit skies, gypsy fires, and flamenco guitars, dancing through the aisles with a Bloody Mary in my hand. I felt a huge pang of loss and suddenly wished I was back behind my stall again, selling tacky lampshades. I felt usurped. Petulantly I agreed with Marcus; the new stall-holder did, indeed, have a long, miserable face.

'I can't believe it was so long ago – all that drama with the Spanish boy. But time and tide, Marcus, it waits for no man,' I said with lament.

'What is this time and tide?'

'Well, it's the idea that man can control many things, but in a way he controls nothing. Time will carry on, and so will the tide and the rolling waves of the sea, long after we're gone. We cannot escape the inevitability, that one day we will no longer be here. Death will catch us.'

'I have no time for this miserable conversation,' Marcus interrupted. 'Anyway, as I was saying, the Iranian. We have slept together, so obviously he isn't that straight.'

'Whatever you do, be careful,' I said. 'Carlos broke your heart.'

'I know, I know. Anyway, how long are you in London for?'

'Only a couple of days.'

'Well, next time you're here, we'll go out with my boring boyfriend for dinner. You will like him; he's more your type. He sits by the fire at night with a book. Always a book. He loves the book.'

Sal came back clutching two polystyrene cups of steaming tea. 'Are you talking about that book of yours again? Ain't you finished yet? It's bloody going on isn't it?'

'I'm nearly there,' I laughed.

'I've heard that before.'

'Anyway, what about you? How are things? How's Jimmy?'

'He's alright,' she said and whisked me away from Marcus's ears into the privacy of the world behind her counter, where only the privileged few had ever set foot.

'And there's no one else? Just Jimmy?'

'Only Jimmy now – no one else. I'm happy with the set up: him in the flat upstairs. Means we can get time apart when we want it. We're not in each other's way all the bloody time, getting under each other's feet. I'm happy with that and I'll keep it like that! What about you? I saw that Ollie on the telly the other night. Did you ever speak to him in the end?'

I didn't contact Ollie again, but I did see him. I bumped into him, a chance meeting in a pavement café on the corner of a street in Soho. He was sitting in the shade of a carousel, rummaging his hands through his hair.

'Ollie,' I said and walked over to his table.

'Hello darling,' he replied, as though we'd arranged to meet here all along.

And perhaps we had. Maybe our souls had arranged to meet again one day, so we could say goodbye on happier ground, or perhaps our pheromones had drawn us together, the scent in the air had felt familiar and unconsciously I'd followed it like a cat winding its way back home. Magic, science, or merely chance, whatever the reason, we spent the afternoon drinking beer and turned our attention to wine as the sky changed from violet to deep midnight blue. The following day was bright again and we spent another night together that led into a week which turned into the whole of the summer.

It was our own private love affair. Nobody knew – only us – and we never told a soul, and neither of us referred to the past. Instead we spent our time dancing to Elvis until dawn, drinking and smoking, laughing and talking, finally healing the wounds of yesterday. It was easy to live in our bubble; we knew each other's oxygen so well. And as easily as we had met, we parted again when the summer was over; our secret summer of love. Instead of diving into nostalgia and despair, we'd bounced on the waves of the present and became what we always were; two free-spirited friends.

But love doesn't end, it just fades, and memories can last a whole lifetime, if you want them to. I still see Ollie every now and then, as distant friends do. A Happy Christmas, an occasional drink, a birthday card here and there. A few weeks ago I met him in a Victorian pub by Liverpool Street. The huge rooms were filled with chatter over lunch and a warm, inviting atmosphere. Ollie had moved to Brighton.

'How is it there?' I asked him.

'It's okay. At first I loved it. In the summer the beaches were crammed full of people. It felt alive. Everyone was so friendly. It was really exciting. But in the winter it was grey and the sea was lonely; it made me feel sad. I decided to never go to the sea again if I felt down, only when I was happy.'

'I know. It can get to you, all that melancholy,' I agreed.

'I saw some amazing seagulls yesterday,' Ollie told me excitedly. 'I went for a walk on the front. I'd never seen so many at once, swooping and swaying, all in unison, like a dance in the air. I caught them on my phone. Do you want to see?'

The sea was light blue and white where the waves broke, frothy furrows in an everlasting field. The gulls above crowed, flying wild. It looked enchanting.

'Come and stay some time,' Ollie said, 'and we can go and look at the sea. It's magical.'

'That would be nice.'

'There's no rush. Whenever you like. She won't be going anywhere.'

'Who's she?' I asked.

'The sea,' he said, 'she doesn't go anywhere. She just keeps moving.'

'It's only us that disappear.'

'Time and tide wait for no man,' Ollie declared.

'I love that phrase too. I use it all the time.'

'Great minds think alike,' he smiled, and we hugged and said goodbye.

I left him at the train station, but I still haven't been to see him or the sea and her magic. But there's magic to be found elsewhere – it's always there if you look for it. It's everywhere if you want it to be. In the pages of books, in the stars that shine on the earth beneath them, illuminating what we need to see. It's in the arms of friends, the friendship of strangers. Even in sadness there is magic, the magic of feeling that the sadness is leaving. Magic is always there if you look for it.

EPILOGUE

It's been thirteen years since I was raped, thirteen years since a small hand took mine at the top of the mountain and led me back through devastation to safety, over rubble and stones, through darkness to light. At times I still feel vulnerable. At times I still feel small, on other occasions I feel valiant, and sometimes I feel grand, but in the end it is the same for everyone. It is life; life is a story. A small moment in time.